Ope

open home

A practical guide to evangelism in the home

Derek Cleave

DayOne

© Day One Publications 2000
First printed 2000

Scripture quotations are from The New International Version.
© 1982 Thomas Nelson Inc.

British Library Cataloguing in Publication Data available
ISBN 1 903087 04 X

Published by Day One Publications
3 Epsom Business Park, Kiln Lane, Epsom, Surrey KT17 1JF.
01372 728 300 **FAX** 01372 722 400
email—sales@dayone.co.uk
www.dayone.co.uk

Designed by Steve Devane and printed by Clifford Frost Ltd, Wimbledon SW19 2SE

Dedication
With gratitude to those who throughout more than thirty years of ministry, have opened their hearts and their homes to a weary itinerant evangelist

Contents

Foreword

On the telephone to a cynical friend of mine, I was told that his church was having its centenary year. "Yes", he said, "we are celebrating one hundred years of keeping the gospel within these four walls."

Derek Cleave, with the other evangelists in 'Christian Ministries' have used homes and food-based events for many of their evangelistic activities. *Open heart, open home* is an explanation of the biblical premise for their emphasis, as well as containing practicalities of what to do, and how to do it well.

Ours is a glorious message. That God our Creator should take the initiative to bring us back to Himself, is worth telling to everyone. Christ was to lovingly bear our sins in His own body on the cross. Having died and been buried, He rose again from the grave. An individual's response to this matters for all eternity. If as Christians we believe this, then we must urgently, by all creative legitimate means, share the message with everyone. The greatest act of friendship is to introduce someone to Jesus Christ.

There is no better way to use our homes, as well as our energy and time, than by setting them aside for God's purposes.

Derek Cleave is an evangelist, and a friend. It has always been a pleasure to have him in our home. If reading this book leads you to opening up your home as a means to evangelism, then Derek, I know, will be delighted.

Roger Carswell

In 1971 I joined the staff of The Movement for World Evangelisation and that neatly coincided with a new dimension in the ministry of that group of evangelists.

A church on Merseyside had invited the entire preaching team for two weeks of mission, majoring in what we have since called 'Hospitality Evangelism.' The concept is very simple and we believe, biblical. It encourages church members to be involved in evangelism by opening not only their hearts but also their homes to unsaved neighbours, friends and work colleagues. Too many Christians then and now, are happy enough with 'Spectator Evangelism' where they can sit on the sidelines and watch others, but they need a push to engage personally with non-Christian, non-church contacts. It is not enough to arrange a rally, invite an evangelist, organise some publicity and hope, even pray, that the people will come. The fact is, many of them won't. I examine some of the reasons for their reticence in the early pages of this book. The Divine commission has always been to 'go **into** the world.' We might discover that this may not be as difficult as we at first imagined.

Today when I am invited to speak at an evangelistic event, I sometimes suggest as an alternative to a formal meeting, perhaps a meal or buffet supper with an evangelistic emphasis. The message will not be compromised in any way, neither in time or content. My suggestion does not mean that I object to preaching rallies, or that I feel the public declaration of the gospel in that way is outdated. I remain convinced of the relevance and importance of preaching and I believe that this can still be effective in a traditional setting with suitable preparation.

However there is a growing section of our community who will not, initially at least, come into that kind of situation. They need a bridge. If we are serious about communicating Christ to others, then making a place in our lives for non-Christian neighbours demands effort, thought, and at times risk. As Haddon Robinson says: 'Bridges are harder to build than walls.' I believe that all effective evangelism is built on relationships. Jesus went out of his way to cultivate relationships. Even if the end objective is getting someone to attend an evangelistic rally, they are still more likely to come as our guest if we have built some kind of meaningful relationship with them.

It is because there are those deterred by traditional settings that I sometimes offer an alternative, which will, I believe, 'guarantee' the attendance of the kind of people we must eventually reach; that guarantee on the understanding that the necessary groundwork is done! The event will still include a thorough presentation of the gospel but it will have the added bonus of the unconverted being present and it will have been preceded by the personal involvement of believers in getting them there. These are just two of the by-products enjoyed when believers are mobilised to this great work of evangelism.

Many years of preparing and speaking at informal evangelistic events have convinced me of their value. They benefit not only those we want to reach but they also provide encouragement for the Christian who really does want to share his or her faith and for whom this may be a first venture into personal evangelism. It is extremely helpful if our first efforts bring a measure of success. That will encourage us to try again.

David Watson quoting Howard Snyder from his book *The Problem of Wineskins* (IVP p. 140) catalogues some of the advantages of these smaller groups to the life and witness of the local church.

'They are flexible, so as to meet changing situations or to accomplish different objectives; they are mobile, going to where the people are, or to where the action is; they are inclusive, demonstrating a winsome openness to people of all kinds; they are personal, offering the best and most thorough form of communication; they can grow by division, multiplying like living cells almost indefinitely without large financial outlays; they can be an effective means of evangelism, offering a natural environment for proclamation and dialogue; they require a minimum of professional leadership, drawing in many who have never known any formal theological training but who, with growing spiritual gifts and constant encouragement, may develop into fine leaders; and they are adaptable to the institutional church—no massive restructuring is required let alone a call to come out of the local church to form yet another church (and probably yet another denomination in due time). Some adjustments will have to be made, no doubt, but none that need threaten the essential life of the local church.' (David Watson, *I Believe in the Church*, Hodder and Stoughton p. 311.)

A number of years ago I spoke at a preparation meeting for a church that was planning a series of home meetings with an evangelistic emphasis. One lady who was present lamented that she was sure no one would respond positively to her invitation. I suggested she should do two things; make an effort and trust the Lord. When I met her again she couldn't wait to tell me about it. Not only had all those she had invited turned up; other neighbours she had left out of the initial invitation had called at her door and asked why they had not been included! That was rather unusual since we can generally count on there being some disappointments; but equally we can be sure that there will also be great encouragements and not a few surprises.

I owe a debt to those whose brains I have picked and whose experiences are shared in these pages. In particular I have leaned heavily on the advice presented by Albert Wollen in his book '*God at work in small groups*' and by Tom Rees in his book '*Breakthrough*' which, though published many years ago, saw the value of the small group long before it reached the popularity it enjoys now. Joe Aldrich's book '*Lifestyle Evangelism*' while dealing with the broader subject of personal evangelism has some very helpful insights into the whole concept of hospitality or friendship evangelism.

I am also grateful to Roger Carswell for so graciously agreeing to write the Foreword. I know of no one who is more committed to reaching the lost with the gospel, and his life and ministry is therefore a constant encouragement to all of us engaged in this work.

Essentially this is intended as a practical book. Fundamentally important matters such as prayer, the content of the gospel and the current spiritual condition of the church are only mentioned in passing because others have written at length on these subjects. When we have examined those areas, there may be issues that need to be dealt with. In the Lord's work the practical can never be truly effective without first laying a good spiritual foundation. When that has been done, the question of 'how' can more readily be addressed. I have used a building analogy in the chapter headings because I believe that evangelism does require thorough preparation and good workmanship, with of course, every aspect immersed in prayer.

I hope therefore, that this book will be sufficiently constructive to prompt some to get involved in the tremendous task of communicating the gospel to men and women in the twenty first century. Many of them will admit to belief in a God yet are ignorant of the glorious truth that the Living God has revealed himself to them in the person of his Son, Jesus Christ.

May God help you to build some bridges, and richly bless you as open, not only your heart but also your home for him.

Derek Cleave
April 2000

There is a legend that recounts the return of Jesus to glory after his time on earth. Even in heaven he bore the marks of his earthly pilgrimage with its cruel cross and shameful death. The angel Gabriel approached him and said, 'Master, you must have suffered terribly for men down there. Do they know about how you loved them and what you did for them?'

'Oh, no,' said Jesus, 'not yet. Right now only a handful of people in Palestine know.'

Gabriel was perplexed. 'Then what have you done to let everyone know about your love for them?'

Jesus said, ' I have asked Peter, James and John and a few more friends to tell other people about me. Those who are told will in turn tell still other people, and the story will be spread to the farthest reaches of the globe. Ultimately, all of mankind will have heard about my life and what I have done.'

Gabriel frowned and looked rather sceptical. He knew well what poor stuff men were made of. 'Yes,' he said, 'but what if Peter and James and John grow weary? What if the people who come after them forget? Haven't you made any other plans?'

Jesus answered, 'I have no other plans. I am counting on them.'

Twenty centuries later, he still has no other plan. He's counting on you and me. High on God's 'To Do' list is the evangelisation of the world. His early disciples adopted his priorities and devoted themselves to reaching their world. Christ counted on them and they delivered. Have we done as well?

(Joe Aldrich. *Lifestyle Evangelism*. Multnomah Publishers Inc. 1981 p. 15).

Viewing the site:
acknowledging where the people are

✪ LOOKING FROM THE OUTSIDE IN

There are some who would say that we are living in a post-Christian society. Speaking at the International Congress for Itinerant Evangelists held in Amsterdam in 1983, Sir Marcus Loane said 'We do not live in a spiritual climate that helps to breed what one might call 'natural Christians.' On the contrary, our long Christian heritage is now threatened with denial and rejection. It is not so much that we live in a post-Christian era; it is rather that we belong to a society which is witnessing the steady erosion of traditional values.' Certainly, church attendance and general knowledge of the Bible by the masses are privileges of the past. Today in some instances, the church is dealing with a third or even fourth generation of absentees.

In contrast, those of us who have maintained an association with the church feel so 'at home' in its surroundings, we can't imagine why others don't feel as we do. Surely, we reason, a warm welcome and an attractive invitation to an evangelistic meeting is all that is required to get a positive response from the invitee. More often than not however, we are met with a polite refusal or a quickly thought-up excuse for not attending, which leaves us wondering why we have been so obviously snubbed.

Of course, a warm invitation and well-produced materials should be characteristics of any church that is efficient and of any church that has a desire to reach others, and sometimes this approach does produce results. More often hundreds or even thousands of pounds are utilised, in the expectation that publicity, literature or some other form of media will work the miracle and 'bring them in' only for us to find it is not as successful as we had hoped. Good Christian literature and video presentations are invaluable in the church's overall programme of evangelism, but these must never become a substitute for real life-changing contact with people. It is often the case that outsiders to faith are first drawn to Christians and then to Christ. This is a principle I will be underlining throughout the book.

Acknowledging a spiritual problem

An unbeliever's negative attitude to any approach from 'the church' has first of all, to be diagnosed from a spiritual perspective. They don't realise it, and would be grossly offended to hear that they are 'powerless', 'ungodly', 'sinners', and 'God's enemies' (Rom 5:6,8,10) and that their attitude to the things of God is part of the evidence of that fact.

Some of us can clearly remember when we had similar feelings towards anything 'religious'. We blamed God and religion for most of the problems in the world and criticised 'the church' for its hypocrisy, until by the grace of God we came to realise that what we saw around us had much to do with what was within us. There was the necessity to re-examine our own nature, and that was the beginning of a life-changing experience. No church programme, however well conceived and executed can, of itself, open spiritually blind eyes. The convicting and converting power of the Spirit of God is the only answer to a rebellious heart.

Addressing the practical problems

Yet while we acknowledge the spiritual condition that is of primary importance, we are not excused from doing everything practical within our power to make the setting for any introduction to Christ and Christian truth appropriate and helpful for the 'outsider' (Col 4: 5). There are some very real problems that unbelievers have in relation to 'the church' in our generation, which at least need to be acknowledged, and in some cases addressed.

Uncertain ground

The church is threatening and uncertain ground for some who have not grown up with it. Even a church building strikes fear into some. I know of several fellowships that have tried to overcome the inhibitions of the world passing its doors by literally opening up the front of their buildings, so that instead of being confronted by a solid wall at the entrance, you can see through glass panels and into the sanctuary itself. This may be only a small step, but it is in the right direction. The church is not a secret society and we should have nothing to hide, so that anything that eases the transition for the visitor has to be of help.

We are occasionally apprehensive when we invite visitors to a church service, but my experience in evangelism has taught me that the average individual is even more fearful when contemplating a visit to church than we ever were in inviting them to come in the first place! I even remember an extreme case of someone taking an overdose of painkillers to avoid having to attend a Christian meeting. We have all listened to Christian testimonies that have invariably included a reference to the initial uncertainty and apprehension felt by those coming from 'outside', simply because of the unfamiliar surroundings they had to confront and overcome. 'Why, when you go to church' I was once asked by a young person, 'do they give you two books (hymn book and prayer book) and why do the people at the front wear dresses?' These examples might seem beyond belief, but equally that kind of response on our part may illustrate just how comfortable we have become in our environment.

Sometimes Christians have not made the transition for the visitor any easier. Pushing songbooks at them, invariably followed by encouragements from the platform to sing enthusiastically, words that they neither understand and certainly have not experienced, can be an excruciatingly embarrassing time for those we have a sincere desire to reach.

Comfortable churches?

Please don't misunderstand me. Ultimately we can't make the church 'comfortable' for the unbeliever. There is something wrong with our church and the message we preach if unbelievers feel comfortable there. But let any offence be the 'offence of the cross' and not that which has been caused by our thoughtlessness.

Equally it **is** important for believers to praise God and to do it well but it is not appropriate or wise for unbelievers to be encouraged to worship when they do not have the essential qualification. God says that those who worship him 'must worship **in spirit** and in truth' (John 4:24) and the unbeliever is incapable of doing that. They can attend a worship service but the worship that Jesus spoke to the woman of Samaria about is worship from the soul. Spiritual worship is effective where the heart is offered to God, and where we do not depend on external forms for acceptance. This is the only worship acceptable to God and the natural man cannot communicate with him in that way (Rom 8:8). We should therefore exercise caution in what we invite unbelievers to do.

So pause and ask the question, 'What is the chief purpose in holding this event in our church?' If our primary intention is to communicate the gospel to **non-church unbelievers** then sometimes it is necessary to move the 'furniture' around or even to remove some of it altogether!

Let's be honest enough to admit that as it stands, the 'person in the pew' has some real difficulties in reaching the 'person in the street' because of 'physical' barriers, whether that barrier be prejudice, ignorance or a brick wall. We must try to see ourselves, as much as possible, as others see us. It might mean we will need to sacrifice some things that suit us. For a while, that will result in **us** being uncomfortable—but in the long run it may help to introduce someone to Jesus Christ.

Irrelevant message?

There is also the difficulty of the **seeming** irrelevance of the church's message. Again there are of course, spiritual reasons for a lack of understanding and appreciation of the gospel. Paul tells us that 'the man without the Spirit does not accept the things that come from the Spirit of God, for they are foolishness to him, and he cannot understand them, because they are spiritually discerned' (1 Cor 2:14). At the same time as we recognise this as a matter of fact for the natural man we are not to despair. God has promised to counter that spiritual blindness with the power of the gospel (Rom 1:16).

A clear message

Even with that provision, the church **as perceived by the world,** seems wonderfully adept at shooting itself in the foot! In presenting its message, the established church often appears to have done more harm than good, and no one denomination is wholly to blame. At different times in its history most sections of the Christian church have been guilty of 'muddying the waters'.

At the Lambeth Conference of the Anglican Church in the late 90's, a number of contentious issues were raised. Serious doubts were being cast by some of the delegates on certain fundamental principles of our faith. The authority and sufficiency of the Scriptures was in question. To counteract this, some of the evangelical African bishops made a statement that provided news for the national press and produced this headline in the Daily Telegraph. 'A hundred years ago you brought us the Bible. Now you are telling us that it is not true!' That was a devastating condemnation of 'the church' as the world sees it. Woolly thinking in relation to fundamental Biblical truths has contributed to the widening gulf between the church and the world.

In the eighteenth century, many including the famous actor David Garrick listened to a particular evangelist. On his way to hear George Whitefield, he bumped into the philosopher David Hume and told him where he was going. 'Why, you don't believe what Whitefield preaches' he said. 'No' said Garrick, 'but he does!' People may not like or even agree with what we are saying but I believe it would help if we were all saying the same thing and with authority! (See Matt 7: 28-29) To enable us to do that we have a canon—a benchmark; it's the Word of God.

More than twenty five years ago I heard David Watson, the late Anglican Bible teacher say that someone had remarked to him that 'the church doesn't scratch me where I itch'. Here was an individual acknowledging some kind of need. He did have an 'itch' but as far as he was concerned the church was unable to offer anything to relieve the irritation. Therefore, presumably he had written 'the church' off. What a tragedy!
I acknowledge that some of the above may be at the extreme end of the scale, but it illustrates the kind of difficulties we have to face in our evangelism.

Good news!

The hymn writer however, was right to declare:
'We have a gospel to proclaim,
Good news for men in all the earth;
The gospel of a Saviour's name:
We sing His glory, tell His worth.'

The church's message is good news! Indeed it's the best news the human ear will ever hear, and primarily because it speaks of the antidote for an individual's greatest problem, that of a broken relationship with his Maker.

The gospel, the message entrusted by God to the church, is as relevant in today's materialistic yet miserable society, as it ever was. But if Paul had to say that he was 'not ashamed of the gospel' (Rom1: 16) it implied that there were those who were!

When the preaching of the gospel is relegated to a secondary position in the programme of any so-called evangelistic event today, it suggests that in some quarters at least, not much has changed! If we have no true gospel or we are ashamed of the one we have, then we should close our doors, because we have downgraded ourselves to little more than mere social clubs, and in many respects the world does better at that than the church.

How then can the church convey its gospel, this 'good-news message' to a world that is suspicious and afraid of what it appears to stand for, and to men and women who don't believe that it has the answers to their questions? Mass evangelism so called, has often been effective in helping the 'fringe', that is those who are already loosely attached to the church perhaps through their family or their own intermittent attendance, but it generally leaves most of the non-religious, non-church persons untouched. To test the truth of that statement, ask yourself this question; 'How many of my neighbours, fellow students, work colleagues or unconverted family members have ever attended a crusade meeting or a gospel rally?'

✪ LOOKING FROM THE INSIDE OUT

The church often gets a bad press, and sometimes from its own members! We should be extremely cautious before we engage in any public criticism of the church. It means a great deal to God. His Son gave his life for it (Eph 5:25), and so the true church is relevant, whatever the world might think. However it's not the bricks and mortar that are important, though within reason these should be cared for. It is the society that God is building, the spiritual church, which is relevant and important and that particular church is made up of people and not inanimate stones (1 Peter 2:5). The theologians call this church the 'invisible' church in the sense that only God sees and knows the exact make-up of its membership, and besides, some of its members already departed from this life **are** invisible to us—at present!

Into the world

The commission to evangelise was given to the portion of that church which remains on earth. Jesus himself said 'As the Father has sent me, I am sending you' (John 20:21). The gospel message therefore, is to be passed on by individuals who by God's grace are members of that society.

In what way is that to be done? Essentially, our lips and our lives are the tools God has given us to carry the message. There must be communication in words from our mouth in order that the message can be heard. But we should also pay heed to our lives, because without the evidence seen there, any words we speak will be built on sand. That will mean that those words though they may contain truth will have no firm foundation and will be dismissed by those who judge us. Those outside of the church can immediately identify a 'credibility gap', which is the difference between what we say with our lips and what we do in our lives. Christians are to be good news before they share the good news. A beautiful bride is the key to evangelism!

Sheldon Vanauken emphasises the point is this way. 'The best argument for Christianity is Christians; their joy, their certainty, their completeness. But the strongest argument against Christianity is also Christians—when they are sombre and joyless, when they are self-righteous and smug in complacent consecration, when they are narrow and repressive, then Christianity dies a thousand deaths.' (*A Severe Mercy*. Harper and Row. 1977. p. 85)

Personal evangelism

Having therefore established that the church of Jesus Christ is the means of communicating the gospel, and that this should be done through life and lip and by the power of the Holy Spirit, without whom we accomplish nothing (John 15:5), what methods are effective and appropriate for our generation?

There should of course be a continuing process of personal evangelism in our daily lives. Some are more gifted at making and using those opportunities than others, but not one member of the church of Jesus Christ is excused from the responsibility of giving 'a reason for the hope that (we) have' (1 Peter 3:15). If this happened more often, then almost certainly we would not need as many of our special programmes.

An Anglican report on Mission in 1974 commented 'for each Christian to help one other to know God and follow Christ would be evangelism on a scale never known in living experience in this country.' This is a challenging assessment that every believer should take to heart.

Joe Aldrich makes a helpful distinction that we would do well to remember. 'Many believers have been burned by an unfortunate experience of attempting to evangelise someone, and they have given up. Often this bad experience is the result of a failure to distinguish between witnessing and soul winning. As long as a man simply tells another about Jesus, he is a witness. But the moment he tries to get that person to do something with Christ, he shifts over to the role of soul winner. Witnessing and soul winning are two different specialities. Many have been taught that evangelism equals soul winning and have tried soul winning with disastrous results. Embarrassed and humiliated, they have withdrawn completely from anything to do with evangelism. (*Lifestyle Evangelism*. Multnomah Publications Inc. 1981. p.18)

Each day should begin with the believer offering himself up to God to be used as his witness through its hours. That day should continue with him looking for God-appointed opportunities to speak for Christ and it will then conclude with gratitude that he graciously answered our prayer. I remember hearing a Christian give testimony to the fact that she had come to faith in Christ late in life. She then challenged the assembled company by asking: 'You might wonder why I never became a Christian before. No one ever spoke to me about Jesus.' How many people with whom I have regularly rubbed shoulders could say a similar thing?

Corporate evangelism

But what of the more specific outreach of the church when it is operating as a body? Some Christians feel that they are not doing the job properly or even 'spiritually' unless the usual religious 'furniture' of the church surrounds them with its formal setting and hymn/prayer sandwich.

I remember many years ago my colleagues and I were suggesting that some churches might consider a change of approach in their evangelistic outreach by adopting a more informal method. This could serve as a vehicle to present the unchanging message in a more suitable way to 'the man in the street'. There were those then who were very uncertain about any change to the established way of doing things. The old system that was familiar to them had 'worked' for many years; therefore it was presumed to be the right and the only way. In any case we are told that 'We were never called to be successful, rather we are called to be faithful'. But 'faithfulness' will include doing God's will in God's way, which may not always equate with our way.

While some churches fail to grow because they do not evangelise, others fail to grow because they do—but in outmoded, ineffective forms. In some cases this can actually hinder the total impact of a church in the community because the effort has not been made to mobilise the **whole** church.

I am convinced that this kind of thinking has contributed to the impasse we are now experiencing. There are unbelievers who will remain ignorant of the gospel because some Christians are only prepared to offer the gospel in a setting familiar to them, yet totally alien to the majority of those we should be reaching. Do we actually recognise what our responsibilities are? Do we really know what evangelism is?

A working definition

Lewis Drummond wrote: 'Evangelism is a concerted effort to confront the unbeliever with the truth about and the claims of Jesus Christ so as to challenge and lead him into repentance toward God and faith in our Lord Jesus Christ and thus into the fellowship of the church.' (Lewis Drummond, *Evangelism ... the counter revolution,* Marshall Morgan and Scott. p. 25)

If we can accept that as a good working definition of evangelism, then notice something very important.

We are to '**confront the unbeliever...**' Evangelism must therefore include

communication to the relevant person or persons. Furthermore, it means that we are not engaging in 'evangelism' as such, if those who need to hear the gospel are not hearing it. If that is true then some of our so-called evangelistic services are not evangelistic at all, though the content of the programme may faithfully present the correct message. Week after week the pastor evangelises the evangelised!

Simple Simon often wondered why he didn't catch any fish from his barrel of water. The reason was obvious to everyone else. There weren't any fish in the barrel in the first place! Paul Little expressed a similar truth in these words. 'The Holy Spirit cannot save saints or seats'. Some churches are like department stores where all the employees arrive at the prescribed time, shut the doors, and then sell merchandise to each other all day.

We must 'confront **the unbeliever**' to be effective as churches in our mission to the world. Every believer loves to hear the gospel but it is good news that must be **shared**. The church supports and cares for its own and rightly so, but there is surely some truth in the words of Archbishop William Temple when he said that the Christian church 'is the only organisation on earth which exists for the benefit of the **non-members**'.

When it comes to methods and practice, there should be, there must be a viable way of introducing those **in our generation** to this unique society and its terms of membership! I believe there is an effective method that is, not surprisingly, a biblical way to introduce the life-changing message of 'the church' to the world and in so doing, to bring them to God.

✪ COMMON GROUND

Over three hundred years ago Judge Edward Coke stated that 'the house of everyone is to him as his castle and fortress.' We have of course paraphrased and popularised that to 'an Englishman's home is his castle.' This is perhaps a shade nationalistic because the same principle is true in any part of the world. The home is considered to be the place where a person should be able to experience the best this world can offer in terms of safety and security. In Eastern Europe during the dark days of communism in particular, many proved this.

Chapter 1

If that is true then the atmosphere of the home should be utilised in the propagation of the gospel. It is an additional tool that most Christians possess but often keep to themselves. The home group is not a substitute for the church, merely an introduction or a first step. For many of those we want to reach, it overcomes the very real fear and trepidation of unfamiliar surroundings and it provides an appropriate setting for the greatest privilege given to us—the declaration of a message that will reconcile a man or a woman to God (2 Cor 5:19-20).

Finding the builder: using what we have, where we are

'Evangelism' is not in the Bible!

In his book '*Urban Harvest*' Roy Joslin makes the very good point that 'Evangelism' is not a Bible word. 'It does not appear in our English versions. Nor is there its equivalent in the original language. So why do we use it? It has to do with spreading the gospel—the 'evangel'. But why is it a word in common usage among evangelical churches today, even though the word does not appear in Scripture?'

Joslin continues, 'It is possible to detect a marked contrast between the New Testament Christians and those of today in relation to the spreading of the gospel. Put simply, it is this: they did it; we talk about it! Evangelism for the early Christians was not something they isolated from other aspects of Christian living in order to specialize, analyse, theorize and organize. They just did it!

Of course, the New Testament contains teaching on the subject of the 'evangel'. It tells us what it is and how we are to spread the good news. But there was never any intention to prepare an 'elite' of keen believers who were 'specially trained' for this Christian activity. In one sense, none of the New Testament believers was a 'specialist' in evangelism; in another sense they all were! It was a part of everyday life for every believer. What is striking about the spreading of the gospel in the New Testament era is the natural way in which this took place' (Evangelical Press p. 79).

Allow me therefore to repeat something I have already stated. It was always the intention of Christ that the church, the whole church, and nothing but the church should be the means for communicating the gospel to the world—and in every generation! (John 20:21).

Does this appear to contradict comments made previously in relation to problems many people have with the church today? Do the 'hang-ups' that many people have, excuse the church from its responsibility in our generation? Did Jesus get the pattern of evangelism wrong for the twenty first century? Does he now have a back-up plan because the church has lost some credibility? The answer in each case is 'no'.

The 'church' as a building is not in the Bible!

Let me make it clear that no biblical reference to a 'church' ever refers to bricks and mortar. Nowhere in the New Testament does the word 'church' refer to an inanimate building. The Greek word for 'church' is formed by combining two words, one meaning 'out from among' and the other the word for 'to call'. In linking them we have the word *ecclesia,* which means 'a called-out assembly or people'. So the true church of God, the biblical church is made up of **people**. It consists exclusively of those who have obeyed God's Word, love God's Son, and have Christ's Holy Spirit living within them.

Therefore that church is in every sense a Living Church with a Living Head (Matt 22:32). Together, these individuals form the body of Christ; he is the One who directs the affairs of his church and as Gavin Reid points out 'being the body of Christ must be viewed in a dynamic way, not a static way. The first body of Christ – Jesus himself, spent no time glorying in his arms and legs and wondering whether they were correctly balanced and linked. He **used** his body to **go** from place to place to teach his message and to die for others' (*To Reach a Nation,* Hodder and Stoughton p.118). So just as different parts of a human body express the personality and feelings of that person, the different parts of the spiritual body of Christ, which together form the Church, are to express him in the world today.

Rubbing shoulders

This leads us to an exciting truth. As much as the world may try to divorce itself from 'the church', due either to misunderstanding or more likely, its own natural alienation from God and the things of God; the world cannot in fact separate itself from the true church. We live in the world and therefore every day believers should be mixing with those we want and need to reach. This is one of the reasons that following conversion we remain on earth in order that we can continue to serve the Lord here by sharing the truth with others. I am sure that angels would be more efficient ambassadors for Christ but they have one great disadvantage. They can never bear witness. They have no personal experience of God's saving grace as we have.

God's means for propagating the message might not be the way we would have planned it, but it is his plan, the only way forward and the unique course of action that will produce eternal results. If you are a Christian, rejoice in that fact and recognise the privilege he has given you to share the truth with others.

✪ SO WHO DO WE KNOW?

When Jesus sent his first disciples into the world, that of course had special relevance for them as the first carriers of the gospel, but it was also to be a pattern for the evangelistic commission given to the whole church. The plan was this. The apostles were to begin where they were in Jerusalem and then extend to the four corners of the earth. But the rapid and far-reaching expansion of the church could not have been the work of this handful of men.

The early chapters of the Acts of the Apostles make it clear that it was often the lay people who were equally active in spreading the gospel. Notice one example of this; 'And Saul was there, giving approval to his (Stephen's) death. On that day a great persecution broke out against the church at Jerusalem, and all except the apostles were scattered throughout Judea and Samaria. **Those who had been scattered** preached the word wherever they went' (Acts 8:1 & 4). The 'professionals' remained behind and the lay people, who were scattered, 'gossiped' the gospel wherever they went.

The emphasis in the original commission was on 'sending' (John 20:21). The word Jesus used has close links with our word for 'missionary'. It definitely implies a 'going'. Jesus never suggested that the usual pattern for world evangelisation would be for the world to come to the church, and in particular at 6.30 on a Sunday evening! The church always goes to the world.

Isolation or separation?

Some Christians have told me without apparent embarrassment that they don't have any friends who are not Christians. Spirituality is sometimes viewed as separation from the unsaved. That attitude does not deserve commendation because that state of affairs has more to do with isolation than separation. 'Many Christians have been so afraid of being contaminated by worldliness that they have avoided any social contacts with unconverted persons. As a result, they have no natural bridge for evangelism; what witnessing they do is usually artificial and forced rather than the spontaneous outgrowth of genuine friendship.'(Leighton Ford. *The Christian Persuaders*. Harper and Row 1966. p. 71-72).

John Stott speaks of a 'rabbit hole Christianity.' The kind who pops his head out of the hole, leaves his Christian home and scurries to his class, only to frantically search for a Christian to sit next to. So he goes from class to class until lunchtime comes when he sits with his Christian friends on one table and thinks 'What a witness!' From there he attends his Christian Bible Study and he might even catch a prayer meeting where the Christians will pray for the unbelievers on his floor. How fortunate he is to live on a floor where there are sixteen Christians! Then at night he scurries back to his Christian roommate. He's safe! He made it through the day and his only contacts with the world were those mad dashes to and from Christian activities. A caricature, yes, but not without some truth.

Believers are familiar with the fact that Christ used the word 'salt' to describe a Christian's effect on the world around him. 'For salt to be effective, it must get out of its container and into the world of hurting, dying, suffering, sinning people. There is no impact without contact.' (Joe Aldrich *Lifestyle Evangelism*. Multnomah Publishers Inc. 1981 p. 19).

There may be a minority of believers who, due to their circumstances, have little or no contact with society but that is certainly not true of the majority. Most of us have neighbours, work colleagues, tradesmen, or unsaved members in our family and they need to hear the gospel. They are our 'Jerusalem'...just as those in the first century had their circle of contacts before moving out to Judea and Samaria and to the ends of the earth' (Acts 1:18). We have no right to deprive them of the opportunity of hearing and seeing the 'good news' by isolating ourselves from them.

✪ WHAT DO WE HAVE?

We are familiar, perhaps over-familiar, with reminders about our Christian stewardship, but we are often slow to use what can be powerful tools in reaching men and women for Christ. When we develop a biblical view of stewardship we view our possessions, few or many, not in the spirit of 'these are mine because I worked for them' but as tools lent for use in Christ's service. I could use my car for transporting people to church, my sports equipment for a neighbour, my crockery and cutlery for a special event, or—my home to provide hospitality. These are instruments we can use in a ministry that will produce benefits that are literally 'out of this world'.

Where better for my unconverted friends to hear the gospel for the first time and be introduced to Christ, than in the surroundings of my home—a Christian home! The gift of hospitality can have explosive evangelistic potential.

✪ USING WHAT WE HAVE FOR WHO WE KNOW

Perhaps our modern Christian society has more difficulty in relating to stewardship than would have been the case for the early church. They were used to the concept of servant-hood, even slavery. The only promotion that a slave could expect was to become a steward, and in the Old Testament Joseph is an example of this. The responsibility of the steward was not to increase his own estate, for he had none, but to use his time and his talents for the entire benefit of his master.

The Christian's ambition as a steward of Christ is to add to the estate of his Master and not to his own. The believer is a purchased possession. Paul makes it clear that there is no getting around this. 'You are not your own; you were bought at a price. Therefore honour God with your body... For he who was a slave when he was called by the Lord is the Lord's freedman; similarly, he who was a free man when he was called is Christ's slave. You were bought at a price; do not become slaves of men (1 Corinthians 6:19-20 and 7:22-23).

It is therefore totally out of place for us to speak in a **possessive** way about, for example, **my** car or **my** home. Rather, in a positive way, we should use those possessions for the benefit of others and the glory of God (See also Leviticus 25:23). To suggest that as Christians, we accept that all these 'things' belong to God and yet never **use** them for him is ignorance at best and hypocrisy at worst.

Once we have come to realise the relevance of Christian stewardship, we say, 'This is not **my** car but yours, Lord. This is not **my** home but yours. All of these are gifts from you and you have given them to benefit your kingdom. How can I **best** use them in your service?'

Hospitality

When it comes to the use of our home, the Christian's response should be one of hospitality. The Scripture makes it clear that for the believer, hospitality is not an option. Paul emphasises the requirement to 'practise hospitality' (Rom 12:13). He also lists hospitality as a necessary gift for high office in the church (1 Timothy 3:2).

Karen Mains in her book *Open heart, open home* (Pickering and Inglis), has carefully distinguished between entertaining and real hospitality. 'Hospitality should not be thought of', she says, 'as a woman's chance to demonstrate her skill in the kitchen and the beauty of her home. Entertaining seeks to impress; hospitality seeks to minister or serve. Entertaining puts things before people. Our concern is more with the home and what our guests will think of it, than with an interest in the people themselves. Hospitality puts aside pride, and Christ is then able to sanctify the most 'ordinary' of homes, making them holy and useful, because the tenants have given themselves and their possessions to him'.

Generally this is an inhospitable world. The philosophy seems to be 'I don't want to bother you and I don't want you to bother me.' The widespread practice of Christian hospitality would do so much to offset this in reaching out to our society. Perhaps that is the reason why some have referred to this more informal approach to evangelism and outreach as 'Friendship Evangelism'.

Breakdown in community

Lewis Drummond identified as one of the difficulties facing the church in the 1970's, the breakdown of community that had led to failure in communications. He wrote then: 'Moreover, the problem is probably going to get worse. The present-day metropolis is giving way to the huge megalopolis. Knowledgeable sociologists inform us that what remnants we have left of community will all but be swallowed up in the new gigantic area-cities that will stretch for hundreds of miles.' What does he suggest to counter this breakdown in community?

'The whole problem for the Church is obviously very complex and deep-seated. One is almost tempted to ask if anything can be done. But perhaps the picture is not quite as dark as may at first appear. I think there is one thing the Church can do that can be of real significance. Now if it has been the breakdown of community that has precipitated our failure in communications, and if the mass-media are largely closed to us, why can we not simply recreate community? If we could do this, we could communicate the gospel in that recreated community. This, I think, is the principle we must grasp if we are to solve our thorny problem. Of course, I know we cannot recreate the social, tribal community as it once was. We cannot turn back the sociological clock. These great movements are certainly beyond us. I do not mean that at all when I speak of recreating community. What I mean is this; why not build little 'communities' through the lives of the church members? Each Christian could become the centre of a 'mini community', as it were. Actually, they already are in one sense. Everyone has his sphere of community, if it is only a few family members and friends. But why could not this circle become enlarged and developed into a sphere of Christian influence and Christian community? If members of the Church could be enlightened to see this and then be led and equipped to build a community around themselves, here would be a tremendous outlet for communicating the gospel. After all, is not this the principle behind the house group, personal evangelism, the all-age Bible study group, etc.? Actually, this is what we were trying to say in the concept of the lay-centred ministry. And I think it is perhaps the most intelligent and relevant way to approach the ministry in the local church in our age' (*Evangelism...the counter revolution*. Marshall Morgan and Scott p.138).

In 1965, in a lecture delivered at Forest Falls, California, Dr. Francis Schaeffer commenting on the future of the church said: 'Unless the church changes its forms and gets back to community and sharing lives personally, the church is done'.

No substitutes

Tom Rees, a great evangelist of a past generation and one who served God during a period when public rallies were an effective means of communi-cating the gospel, wrote, 'Alas there are many well-meaning Christian people who spend much of their time at crusades, conventions, Bible studies and prayer meetings, who think only of evangelism in terms of big meetings, who never raise a finger to help the needy folk next door but will suddenly start plastering posters everywhere and booking coaches for the Royal Albert Hall or Earls Court and wonder why so few people show any interest and fewer still turn to the Lord . . . Mass evangelism when divorced from disciplined prayer and Christian kindness towards individuals is both unbiblical and abortive' (Tom Rees, *Breakthrough,* Hildenborough Hall p. 128). He is making clear the fact that even in an age when public meetings were a more acceptable format for propagating the gospel, there was still no substitute for a spirit of hospitality.

In Webster's Dictionary, the definition for *hospitable is* wedged between the word *hospice,* which is a shelter, and the word *hospital*, which is a place of healing. As Karen Mains points out, 'Ultimately this is what we offer when we open our homes in the true spirit of hospitality. We offer shelter; we offer healing . . . the model for entertaining is found in the slick pages of women's magazines with their appealing pictures of foods and rooms. The model for hospitality is found in the Word of God.'

'In' but not 'of'

Sadly, many Christians have isolated themselves from a world that is suffering and that is in direct contravention to our Lord's command: 'Go **into** all the world and preach the good news to all creation' (Mark 16:15 see also John 17:18).

Believers have been warned, and rightly so, about the dangers of socialising with the world and that caution certainly needs reiterating in our generation, but there is a vital difference between separation and isolation. Jesus made the difference very clear when he prayed to his Father, 'My prayer is not that you take them out of the world but that you protect them from the evil one. They are not of the world, even as I am not of it. Sanctify them by the truth; your word is truth' (John 17:15-17).

Identifying with the world is not the same as being identical to it. Christ was a friend of sinners but he was not a sinner. He had a radical identification with the world but he was also radically different from the world. It was one of the reasons for his effectiveness. We are **in** the world because Christ wanted it that way, but like him we are not **of** the world. We are to be distinct and different but not remote and inaccessible.

The isolation ward in a hospital is there in order to stop germs spreading. The obvious way to stop the spread of the gospel is to isolate the 'carriers'. Perhaps this accounts for so much of our ineffectiveness in reaching the world for Christ.

Looking at the blueprint:
principle and pattern

✪ IN THE NEW TESTAMENT

Anumber of years ago I was outlining the principles of 'Hospitality Evangelism' at a church just north of London. In particular I emphasised the possibility of using the home to invite friends and neighbours to a hearing of the gospel. I was getting rather excited about my ideas when someone took the wind from my sails by remarking, 'There's nothing new in that. They did it in that way in the New Testament!'

Of course, I knew that; at least, I think I did—but immediately I saw clearly that not only do we have the **principle** of hospitality evangelism presented in the Word of God, we also have the **pattern** repeated over and over again in its narratives.

Later church history also confirms the vital role the home has played in Christ's work in building his church. Let's be clear, therefore, that using the home for God is no twentieth or twenty first century innovation. It is as old as Christianity and very obviously initiated by Christ himself.

Whilst our Lord constantly preached in the open air, his evangelism in depth, his instruction classes and, particularly, his teaching of the disciples, was often conducted in a private home. (See, for example, Matthew 13:36; Mark 9:28). Matthew himself 'held a great banquet for Jesus at his house' (Luke 5:29). Mark, recording the same event, says that 'Many tax collectors and "sinners" were eating with him and his disciples' (Mark 2:15). This was not primarily for entertainment but rather hospitality that included direct evangelism. I cannot imagine that the Lord, nor even Matthew, missed the opportunity to share the good news of God's forgiveness with this diverse crowd of human beings (see Matthew 9:11-13).

Another tax collector, this time in Jericho, used his home to provide a platform for Jesus to preach to his family and friends (Luke 19:5-6). Zacchaeus gave his testimony and Jesus preached the message of salvation (Luke 19:9-10). The Lord uses what we have. He didn't ask the same of the blind beggar, who could not have provided the kind of affluence Zacchaeus enjoyed (Luke 18:35-43). The principle never changes: God never asks of us what he has not seen fit to give us, but he always expects to use what we have been given.

And so the pattern continues throughout our Lord's earthly ministry until the final hours when again he chose the privacy of a house for his farewell to his disciples (Luke 22:11). As Tom Rees says, 'the Son of God was born in a borrowed manger, buried in a borrowed tomb, and did much of his teaching in borrowed homes' (Tom Rees, *Breakthrough*; Hildenborough Hall).

...To be continued

Jesus obviously intended that the apostles should continue in the same vein in order that the gospel should be spread. He not only gave them the message but also provided practical instruction as to their technique (see Matthew 10:11-14). It was quite natural that having seen the Lord work so effectively in both the open air and in the home, wherever people gathered and were willing to listen they followed suit.

In addition of course, there was the prevailing climate of the day. In a word, persecution. In the earliest days of the Christian church, the apostles openly stood in the temple area and preached Christ. Then they were forbidden to do this but continued until Peter was thrown into prison. He was miraculously released and went back to the same area yet again. Taken before the Sanhedrin they were instructed not to preach or teach in the name of Jesus but the record states:

'The apostles left the Sanhedrin, rejoicing because they had been counted worthy of suffering disgrace for the Name. Day after day, in the temple courts **and from house to house**, they never stopped teaching and proclaiming the good news that Jesus is the Christ' (Acts 5:41-42).

Eventually believers were persecuted so severely that they had to move, not only from the temple courts but also from Jerusalem itself, so fulfilling our Lord's commission to spread out from that centre (Acts 1:8). As they moved away from the temple they used the local synagogues in various towns, until those who had resisted them in Jerusalem persuaded the locals to do the same.

Paul was often barred from the synagogue and many of the apostles were beaten (see Acts 13:50, 14:19). They then made use of the market place, or 'agora', where people were gathered together and provided a ready-made congregation.

However, alongside this varied and troubled public ministry, there was the ongoing ministry in the home. Therefore from choice and sometimes out of necessity, the hospitality evangelism of their Lord continued. So severe were the pressures and so ostracised the believers, the Christian church as a group met in private homes. The Acts of the Apostles and the epistles are full of such references. See, for example, Romans 16:5; 1 Corinthians 16:19; Colossians 4:15; Philemon v. 2.

The pattern of Paul

When founding the church in Philippi, Paul used the homes of a businesswoman, Lydia, and the town jailer (Acts 16:14-15, 32). In Corinth, he used the home of his hosts Aquila and Priscilla, and apparently declared the gospel in the house of Justus (Acts 18:1-3, 7-8). When he recounted his ministry in Ephesus, he reminded them not only of his message but also of his technique. 'You know that I have not hesitated to preach anything that would be helpful to you but have taught you publicly **and from house to house.** I have declared to both Jews and Greeks that they must turn to God in repentance and have faith in our Lord Jesus' (Acts 20:20-21).

And Paul never changed his tactics—as long as he could he discharged this twofold ministry and when the public ministry was halted, he continued in private. When he was delivered under guard to Rome he was given lodgings, with a soldier to watch over him, and we are told that the people 'came in large numbers to the place where he was staying. From morning till evening he explained and declared to them the kingdom of God and tried to convince them about Jesus from the Law of Moses and from the Prophets. Some were convinced by what he said, but others would not believe' (Acts 28:23-24). The Word of God says that they '**would** not believe', not that they 'could' not. Their failure had more to do with disobedience than disability. That is to be deplored rather than pitied. We should remember that in our own evangelism today.

The final verses of the Acts tell us that, 'For two whole years Paul stayed there in his own rented house and welcomed all who came to see him. Boldly and without hindrance he preached the kingdom of God and taught about the Lord Jesus Christ' (Acts 28:30-31).

The use of the home in teaching and evangelising was therefore not only the Lord's pattern but also that of the apostles.

✪ ... IN CHURCH HISTORY

History bears continuing testimony to the value of the home. David Watson in his book, *I Believe in the Church,* writes: 'the spiritual momentum of the Reformation was in large measure spurred on by the emphasis on small group Bible studies. The same was true of the Wesleyan revival in the eighteenth century—and the astonishing spread of the Pentecostal church, especially in Latin America, could never have happened without this same pattern of the small group' (p. 311).

Seventeenth century

One of the greatest examples of the value of the 'house-to-house' technique comes to light in the ministry of Richard Baxter (1615-1691). Baxter's public preaching was greatly blessed but he is particularly remembered for his emphasis on the spreading of the gospel through his visitation of the homes in the parish of Kidderminster. He shares his views on evangelism from house to house:

'I know that preaching the gospel publicly is the most excellent means because we speak to many at once. But it is usually far more effectual to preach privately to a particular sinner, as to himself; for the plainest man that is, can scarcely speak plain enough in public for them to understand; but in private we may do it much more. In public we may not use such homely expressions or repetitions, as their dullness requires, but in private we may. In public our speeches are long and we overrun their under-standings and memories and they are confounded and at a loss and not able to follow us, and one thing drives out another and so they know not what we said. But in private, we can take our work gradually, and take our hearers along with us; and, by our questions and their answers we can see how far they understand us, and what we have next to do. In public, by length and speaking alone we lose their attention but when they are interlocutors (when they take part in the conversation) we can easily cause them to attend. Besides, we can better answer their objections and engage them by promises, before we leave them, which in public we cannot do. I conclude therefore, that public preaching will not be sufficient; for though it may be an effectual means to convert many, yet not so many as experience and God's appointment of further means may assure us.'

He adds this comment: 'I wonder at myself, how I was so long kept off from so clear and excellent a duty ... Whereas, upon trial, I find the difficulties almost nothing (save only through my extraordinary bodily weakness) to which I imagined; and I find the benefits and comforts of the work to be such, that I would not wish I had forborne it, for all the riches in the world. We spend Monday and Tuesday, from morning almost to night, in the work, taking about fifteen or sixteen families in a week, that we may go through the parish, in which there are upwards of eight hundred families, in a year; and I cannot say yet that one family hath refused to come to me, and but few persons excused themselves, and shifted it off. And I find more outward signs of success with most that do come, than from all my public preaching to them. I have found by experience, that some ignorant persons, who have been so long unprofitable hearers, have got more knowledge and remorse of conscience in half an hour's close discourse, than they did from ten years public preaching' (Richard Baxter, *The Reformed Pastor*, Banner of Truth p. 196-7).

The seventeenth century therefore saw the value of using the home to reach the community.

Eighteenth century

Roy Joslin gives us this insight into the eighteenth century:
'During the following century the advance of the gospel gained a new impetus with the advent of the Evangelical Awakening. Writing of the conditions which prevailed as the century drew to a close, a leading Particular Baptist, John Rippon, drew attention to the way in which public proclamation of the gospel was being suitably complemented by the private opportunities for further biblical instruction. After Sunday afternoon services in their own chapels, multitudes of men were dispersed among the villages. In the gospel witness that took place, some would lead

the singing and others would preach or read specially written 'village sermons'. When a village community showed signs of response, prayer meetings and 'village readings' were arranged. These were often held on mid-week evenings in the cottage of some person who had displayed special interest. These cottage meetings formed the basis of numerous Nonconformist congregations. John Rippon reckoned that "the whole country was open for village preaching in the 1790's"' (*Urban Harvest* Evangelical Press).

Class meetings

In the same century, John Wesley recognised the worth of small groups through the Methodist Class Meetings: 'It may well have been that his mother's weekly talks with the children convinced John that the opportunity for fellowship is essential to the Christian, and thus led indirectly to the formation of the Holy Club at Oxford and, later, of the class meeting in Methodism. The gatherings she held at the rectory (begun whilst Samuel was attending Convocation in 1712) may equally have brought to John's notice the value of such groups to supplement the normal services of the Church, and thus have paved the way for the founding of his societies. In the absence of the Rector, there was no afternoon service, and the curate was a dull, unevangelical preacher whose monotonous theme was the duty of paying debts. In these circumstances, Mrs. Wesley was led to hold an informal meeting in her kitchen on Sunday evenings, primarily for her family and the servants. But soon others begged to come, and over two hundred people were crammed into the room. Young John, now approaching the age of nine, and mature beyond his years, must have taken all this in. Little did he suspect that such a scene was to be repeated in his own ministry on scores of occasions in his own itinerant ministry' (*The Burning Heart*. A Skevington Wood. Paternoster p. 31).

Dating from the early organisation of Methodism in 1742, the Class Meeting was part of John Wesley's policy to increase understanding of the faith and to ensure growth in holy living. Members of each local society were divided into groups that met weekly under a lay reader for 'fellowship in Christian experience.'

Skevington Wood continues 'In Wesley's eye this was the keystone of the entire Methodist edifice. At first Wesley attempted to examine the classes himself, but soon he had to delegate the supervision to leaders, and thus the organization of under-shepherds to the flock was inaugurated. As a system of pastoral care, especially for the newly-converted, it was ideal. The class was the disciplinary unit of the society. It was the responsibility of a leader "to see each person in his class, once a week at least, in order to inquire how their souls prosper; to advise, reprove, comfort, or exhort, as occasion may require; to receive what they are willing to give toward the relief of the poor." He also kept the preacher informed as to the sick, or the disorderly. Thus "evil men were detected, and reproved. They were borne with for a season. If they forsook their sins, we received them gladly; if they obstinately persisted therein, it was openly declared that they were not of us. The rest mourned and prayed for them, and yet rejoiced, that, as far as in us lay, the scandal was rolled away from the society".'

Nineteenth and twentieth century

The nineteenth century and, in particular, the Welsh revival with its cottage prayer meetings, followed the pattern, and the twentieth century, in a remarkable way, came alive to the possibilities of a similar technique.

The last century saw East European believers facing persecution for their faith from atheistic communism. Many of these, unable to meet publicly, continued to grow numerically and spiritually because of the value of meetings in the home. There is similar pressure today in other parts of the world for a variety of reasons, and we may move into a period when even in the West we are unable to enjoy the liberty and privilege of our present freedom. The institutional church might be threatened, but what history shows us is that 'the church-in-the-home can survive anything!' (Albert Wollen. *God at work in small groups,* Scripture Union p. 39).

I believe that this twenty first century will be no exception. Howard Snyder, in his book, *The Problem of Wineskins,* believes that: 'A small group of 8 to 12 people meeting together informally in homes, is the most effective structure for the communication of the gospel in modern secu-lurban society' (IVP p. 139).

Luis Palau comments: 'All around the world God is using home Bible study groups to bring new life and growth to his church. From Korea to

Brazil and China to North America people have been swept into the kingdom of God as a result of small groups sharing together around the Bible'.

None of this overturns the traditional means of preaching the gospel. It will still be preached within the congregation of God's people gathered for worship (1 Cor 14:24-25) and that will inevitably mean that it will also be preached to unbelievers. As long as there are church buildings there will be an essential place for preaching the gospel but we do need to recognise that the **evangelistic** opportunities in some of those situations will vary considerably.

Laying the foundations:
the church in the home

In Christianising the empire around AD 300, the Emperor Constantine dealt the church a severe blow. Everyone would now be called a Christian whatever their spiritual condition. Never was the phrase 'nominal Christian' more apt. Ecclesiastical buildings were rapidly constructed and the church became an institution. Yet significantly this period is known as the Dark Ages because the church lost its way.

This together with all that has been said previously about the communication level of the church today would seem to suggest that the quicker we get rid of the institution the better. But that is not the answer.

Let Albert Wollen make the point: 'I don't believe that the institution is, of itself, the problem. The downfall is that we lost a dimension under institutionalism that needs to be restored to the church. We need to bring the church back to the place where the people within the institution are closely related to one another in fellowship and true community. We must help people find their way back to interaction with each other in terms of their faith and building up their lives personally around the Word of God.' (*God at work in small groups*. Scripture Union).

The last two sentences are particularly relevant. Though this book aims in particular to provide information that will help in using the home with **evangelism** in mind, we should emphasise the importance of the small group in building up the body of Christ for the work of ministry.

✪ RENEWED RELATIONSHIPS

Some years ago my wife and I were invited to a church member's home for the evening. About six or eight others were also present. The evening was not structured but we talked together about the sort of things Christians should talk about. I was brought up in the same church as most of them, yet we realised that after forty or more years of attending church services together we didn't really know much about each other! We were strangers but didn't realise it until we began to interact.

This suggests that the home could feature as much for the benefit of believers, as for reaching out to the unbeliever. The biblical pattern we reviewed earlier always began with the believers, though sometimes the lines were not drawn too strictly. Meetings planned with believers in mind, can sometimes be of help to unbelievers. The Spirit of Christ is perfectly able to apply the truth of the Scriptures to a mixed audience and in a variety of ways.

Fellowship

As believers we benefit from the help that Christian fellowship can bring to our lives. If for a moment you doubt that, then ask someone who through illness or duty has been deprived of that contact for any period of time. God is a firm believer in the family unit and emphasises its value not only in the natural family but also in the spiritual one, since the church is in effect an extended family. However the regular and formal programme of many churches does not always make it easy for us to experience real fellowship, though we often suggest that is what we are doing when the teapot comes out!

There may be some who will recoil from the concept of getting closer together, because it doesn't suit their nature; they prefer to remain on the perimeter of church activities. Sadly, when that happens everyone is the loser. 'No man is an island' wrote John Donne and if a believer insists on trying to be one, then the Christian family as a body will suffer.

Pagan contemporaries of early century believers were amazed at the love Christians had for each other. If that was true then, surely there is no reason why something similar will not hold true in the twenty first century. That would certainly be in stark contrast to the society we live in today. Humankind, certainly in our Western society, likes to think of itself as caring and compassionate and large amounts of money are donated to worthy charities year on year. However, I believe that this camouflages the true picture.

The good cause

The National Lottery donates a percentage of its profits to charity in an effort to justify its existence, but I have to ask why people need the incentive of winning something for themselves in order to prompt them to give to those in need. Raffle tickets have often been thrust in my direction on a similar premise– 'It's for a good cause.' If it is, and if we are a caring and compassionate society, as we like to think we are, then I will want to give without any thought of return or reward.

The bottom line is this: it may sadden us but should not surprise us to realise that people are primarily motivated by self-interest. It should not surprise us because that is the biblical diagnosis of our nature. Self-centredness is a characteristic of sin (see Isaiah 53:6) and since we are all sinners then our natural and number one concern will be for ourselves. But this is where the contrast should be seen.

The Christian is different and in the first century those outside of the faith recognised a new character trait. They saw that the followers of Christ really loved each other and were prepared to put others first, even to the extent of laying down their lives for one another. How was this possible? The Scriptures tell us that they were able to do that because of the love that Christ by his Spirit had put there (Rom 5:5). God's love has been 'poured into our hearts.' That suggests an inundation with the resultant overflow that should ultimately benefit others. The world will listen when Christians love.

Love your neighbour

The capability that the believer has to love both those inside and outside of the family of God is not something that has been attached to them by an outside source. An outside source doesn't attach fruit that appears on a natural tree. The fruit appears spontaneously from within the plant. In a similar way Christian love comes only from the indwelling Spirit of God. It is part of the fruit of the Spirit and cannot be engineered or counterfeited. It is nothing less than God's love flowing out from the indwelling Spirit. One of its significant characteristics is that it goes out to objects of Divine, rather than natural, affection.

This selfless love is cultivated by an ongoing relationship with Christ (John 15:4). A key word in this passage is the word 'abide' (A.V.) or 'remain' (N.I.V.). The word 'abide' is repeated ten times in verses 4-10. The metaphor of the vine illustrates the point; it is only when nutrients flow freely that fruit can be borne, and part of that fruit is love. Expressing this within the body of Christ is much more effective in witnessing to our contemporaries than simply 'going to church'. Jesus never said 'All men will know that you are my disciples, if you meet on Sundays at 11.00 am and 6.30 pm.' He made it absolutely clear when he said, 'All men will know that you are my disciples **if you love one another**' (John 13:35). God's love expressed between believers is the unique badge of discipleship. So don't run away from opportunities to experience and enjoy Christ's love with brothers and sisters in God's family. Interaction and expressions of the reality and practicality of our faith are important to a healthy spiritual life and as a bonus they will prove to be an effective witness to the world.

✪ THE HOME FELLOWSHIP GROUP: PLANNING

The home fellowship group can be a real means to this end. Since it is part of the ongoing life of the church it is important if at all possible, to have support from the leadership of the church. If the pastor or church leader is not the initiator he should certainly be consulted in the early days of praying and planning. Any minister who loves the Lord and the Lord's people is going to thank God that his members are meeting in their homes to read the Scriptures and pray.

There are dangers of course, as there will be in any situation where you allow individuals a measure of freedom. Your minister may want to discuss certain matters with you, such as the leadership of the groups, the programme envisaged, and what the time-commitment might be for those involved. This is quite understandable and should not be considered as interference. The minister has to have the good of the whole congregation at heart and must be sure that the end result of this will be beneficial to the entire church. If of course, the home fellowship or Bible study groups are an official church activity, then the minister should have overall leadership of these and he will be responsible for their development. It will be wise in either case to run them on an experimental basis for a period of say, three or six months, with the situation reviewed at the end of that period.

Benefits and hazards

Many ministers see the value of these groups to the total ministry of the church. Some have been brave enough to insert small group study in homes in the place of perhaps up to three mid-week meetings per month. One church, which was getting about thirty to the Bible study, has now increased its weekly average to over 150 by holding some of these in homes. Numerically this has to be a good thing but you should also be aware of some of the risks.

The minister's position means that he has overall responsibility in that church for the teaching of its members. If the groups are too many and the leadership of the groups so varied, he can lose touch with what many would consider his prime responsibility, which is the feeding and teaching of the people. In short, he doesn't know what is going on! He has lost a measure of control in that specific area in which he is responsible to God. These are days of 'team ministry', which has much to commend it, but in this essential area of teaching someone has to accept the final responsibility. That person is the minister or teaching elder (James 3:1).

To counteract this problem some ministers, having very carefully chosen their group leaders, will then meet with them and determine the direction that the groups should take. This does help to protect the material that is discussed. The word 'discussed' highlights another concern that should be recognised.

Discussed or proclaimed?

If house groups are held to the exclusion of public meetings, then the Word of God is often discussed but not as often taught, and that cannot be a good thing. It should not be necessary for me to underline the primacy of preaching i.e. the public declaration of the Word of God, which is so clearly underlined and illustrated in the Scriptures. Discussing the Word of God can be a profitable activity but it should never be a substitute for hearing it taught. Paul wrote 'How can they believe in the one of whom they have not heard? And how can they hear without someone preaching to them?' (Rom 10:14).

So house meetings whether for believers or unbelievers should always be regarded as supplementary to what we might call the 'traditional' or established ministries of the church.

Another threat we face is the fact that it is possible for a meeting in a home to exaggerate the very problem it seeks to address. Small groups offer the potential for a limited number of individuals to get to know each other really well. The danger is that we exclude ourselves from getting to know others in the wider fellowship of our church. To deal with this potential difficulty some churches have changed the make-up of the groups from time to time to give a different mix.

If we are using the family home, what do our families think about it? The decision to open a home for small group Bible study and fellowship should ideally be a family one. Certainly husband and wife should agree on this intrusion. Nor will it create the best atmosphere if other members of the family feel invaded because they were not aware of this new change. Our children, if we have them, should be welcomed into the groups themselves, to encourage this approach in their own lives in later years. If we keep our front door shut, then they are likely to do the same.

✪ THE HOME FELLOWSHIP GROUP: LEADERSHIP

As I have already indicated, leadership of small groups is vitally important. This is not a situation in which we call for volunteers. The minister or church elders should be involved in selecting those who are most suitable. This may help to allay any fears that the leadership of the church might have, and it should produce the right calibre of person.

Gifts of leadership

The leader will be spiritually mature and emotionally secure. It is also important that he or she should lead! Leadership of a group has more to it than opening in prayer and announcing the first question. He should be sensitive as to when the group needs some input and when to hold back. He need not be trained theologically but it is essential that he has some experience as a student of the Bible. In the context of home Bible study he is not there to preach. He is there to do his learning with the group. He will not dominate the group with his own personality but will do what he can to make sure that the group is Christ-centred. The individual may not even consider himself leadership material but will be the type who can draw out others because of his approach. He will never be rude though he may need to be firm. There will always be the over-talkative member! One of his greatest gifts if the discussion tends to wander, will be his ability to put it back on the right lines. It is also important that he is seen to have the respect of the minister and church leaders and that in turn he respects them.

Consultation

As I have suggested there is obviously great value in the minister meeting with the leaders to discuss the material to be studied. Subject matter can sometimes be chosen that would be divisive and this should be avoided, certainly in the early days. The minister will also want to know how the groups are progressing and what conclusions have been reached. By meeting regularly in this way, the minister can be more aware of what is happening in the groups and deal with any problems as they arise. The conduct of the group meeting will vary and it would be impossible to standardise in these pages. However the following ideas may be helpful as a guide.

✪ THE HOME FELLOWSHIP GROUP: STRUCTURING THE EVENING

It doesn't take many to get a class started; three or four would be sufficient, with six to ten ideal. Don't be surprised if only a few are prepared to commit themselves at the beginning; others will join as the scheme gains momentum. Only light refreshments should be served and these need not appear until the end of the evening, unlike an evangelistic situation where coffee and biscuits can help to serve as an 'ice-breaker' when guests arrive. Chairs should be arranged informally with the leader's place situated so that he can see and be seen. The chairs should not be put in rows as in a meeting, though some groups find it helpful to sit around a table that can be used for taking notes. Make sure the room is comfortably heated and ventilated and that sufficient Bibles are available, though in this situation one would hope that Christians would have brought their own.

The evening will usually begin with prayer and the leader might select someone to take this. If the group are meeting specifically for Bible study, then singing might be omitted. The leader will introduce the passage to be studied and may not take more than a few minutes in doing this. He will have prepared some background material to the book or character being studied, but this is not primarily an occasion for him to teach so his introduction will be brief. The evening will then be open for discussion and the leader will seek to structure this, rather than merely asking if anyone has anything to say.

If a passage is being studied, it may be helpful to read it in more than one version of the Scriptures. Identify those that are true translations and those that are paraphrases and explain the difference.

Where to begin

In the early stages as members are feeling their way it might be advisable to tackle one of the Gospels. Questions then need to be asked about the passage. Albert Wollen shares the very simple procedure he has seen adopted with some success.

What Does the Bible Say?

To begin the class the leader calls for a volunteer or names someone in the group to read the section of verses. The leader should not name someone to read until it is obvious the person is perfectly free and willing to be called upon in that manner. He or she must be sensitive and never offend or lead in such a way that might cause a person to clam up, withdraw from the activity or stop sharing in the class.

The paragraph or section of verses may be read in any version depending on the volunteer. After the reading of the paragraph, the leader launches a question regarding what the text says. As the group responds, the leader makes sure the group stays with the biblical text. After the leader has launched the question he should guide the group's discussion of that question. Then when he feels there has been sufficient discussion, he should smoothly summarize the response and lead into the next question.

It usually requires a series of questions to adequately bring to light the content of the passage. But at no time should the leader feel responsible to answer the question he has launched. Nor should he allow himself to answer side questions that someone may raise, for in so doing he may inadvertently divest the Scripture of its authority and assume the authority role himself. The Scripture should always answer for itself.

Although someone may feel a particular truth should be stressed, no unusual emphasis should be placed on that truth. Rather, leaders should let self-evident truths rise naturally from the discussion. There may also be a tendency for some Christians to try to establish their particular views on certain scriptural points and disprove the views of others. A wise leader will draw the discussion graciously back to the text itself and again ask, "What does the text say?" This will avoid the extravagances of individual interpretation upon the text.

What Does It Say to Me?

After a sufficient time is spent discussing the content of the text the leader puts forth the question, "What does it say to me?" The personal application is necessary if there is going to be any meaningful dialogue in the group. Discussion does not imply dialogue. One may discuss at length any subject without any personal involvement with the subject of the discussion. Not until the subject matter has been exposed to the human personality and personally applied can real dialogue begin to take place. The leader's role here is to encourage individuals to respond to the content in terms of their personal experiences (*God at work in small groups.* Scripture Union. p. 87).

An example

The experience of Helen as she saw this take place in one of her classes is testimony to its effectiveness.

"We opened the Bible, and we asked two simple questions: 'What does it say?' and, 'What does it say to me?' Later my first class suggested that we add another question: 'What does it say to me for today, for this specific day?' Then towards the end of the year they wanted to add another one: 'How did it change my life last week?' It was changing their lives. It was changing my life too. We learned to listen to each other—not just to words, but also to the lives behind the words. In listening to others I found that my own need was being voiced and met also. We allowed everyone to state their own opinions, and they were able to do this without defence. I think it is very necessary to create this freedom within the group. The natural response to listening to each other is to open God's Word and listen to it. To me this is true dialogue, sharing lives with each other around the Word, then relating the truth from God's Word and appropriating it for our needs. We allowed the Bible to speak for itself. You can't go wrong with this rule. I didn't need to interpret it for the group. I felt the Holy Spirit was fully adequate to do this".

There are several courses for Bible study that have proved very effective in stimulating a group.
You may care to contact the following for details:

❯ St Matthias Press, P O Box 665, London SW20 8RL.
E-mail mattmedia@compuserve.com
❯ *'Finding out about Christ'* Workbooks from Edward Challen,
642 Ringwood Road, Parkstone, Poole,
Dorset, BH12 4LZ.

Alternatively, the minister or teaching elder could set questions for discussion by all the home groups.

Bible Meditation card

As a third option, something like a Bible Meditation card can be equally useful in the group situation as it is for the individual. This card poses certain questions that the leader can use:

- ■ What is the main truth of this verse?
- ● What other Scripture can I find to illuminate this verse?
  (Look up the references given in the margin of your Bible).
- ■ Is there any word or part of this verse that I do not understand?
- ● Is there a command, or word of advice, here to obey?
- ■ Is there a good example to follow?
- ● Is there a sin or mistake to avoid?
- ■ Is there a warning to heed?
- ● Is there a promise to claim?
- ■ Is there a prayer to echo?
- ● How can I see my own experience reflected here?
- ■ How can I apply this Scripture to practical, everyday life?
- ● How can I turn this verse into prayer?

This will invariably open up the passage to the group, who will relate it to the practical realities of life, and in so doing, will share with each other in a way that is not possible through a monologue.

The leader may try to draw out timid members of the group, by asking for contributions from anyone who has not already spoken. It is important however that no one is pressurised. Some groups limit their discussion time to one hour and find that this is a useful discipline.

It is helpful to conclude the evening with prayer, relating the prayers in particular to what has been learnt. Perhaps this would be a time for the group to share other items for prayer as appropriate.

The Bible Meditation card has the following challenge on its reverse side:

The success of this group Bible study depends on me

I can help most by:

- ■ Praying earnestly for God's blessing on others, the leader and myself.
- ● Depending upon the Holy Spirit to illuminate the Scriptures.
- ■ Looking to God to speak to me personally.
- ● Approaching the Bible in true humility, not to criticise but to be criticised by God's Word.
- ■ Avoiding preaching sermonettes to the Group.
- ● Endeavouring to participate whenever I can in sharing thoughts or by asking questions.
- ■ Not monopolising the Study in talking too much.
- ● Giving loyal support to the leader and encouragement to others.
- ■ Being ready, with grace and humility, to agree to differ from others.
- ● Never discussing adversely the leader or other members of the Group in their absence.

As I have already said, group Bible study is no substitute for either the public exposition of the Scriptures, or our own personal study of God's Word. It should, however, be a stimulus to both. This sort of programme will prepare believers to share in personal relationships and spiritual concern for each other, which can be fertile ground into which the unbeliever can be introduced.

This might be the moment to reaffirm our confident trust in the power and authority of God's Word whether presented to benefit believers or unbelievers. When men and women interact with its truths, things begin to happen…often unexpected things. As Joe Aldrich says 'Unbelievers find themselves at the foot of the cross and wonder how they got there.' (*Lifestyle Evangelism*. Multnomah Publishers Inc. 1981. p.165)

Divide and multiply

It will be helpful for a group to divide and multiply, but not too quickly. Assuming that they meet weekly, the nucleus should remain together for a number of months in order that a strong level of trust can be formed. However, new blood must be introduced and eventually this will mean division into other cells, which will need to be handled sensitively. I know of one group that has divided but have been able to do that in the same home, so that their study and prayer are conducted independently but they meet together for coffee at the end of the evening. This will not always be possible but it helps to smooth over what can be an awkward transition. New leadership material will become obvious as the weeks go by, so that the new group can have one of its existing members as its new leader.

Wise use of the small group for Bible study and prayer can have a very real impact on the life of the church. Many of those who previously had been spectators, become active members. Some, who were never before given positions of leadership and who, perhaps, never sought for them, blossom into vital members of the fellowship. The church is now becoming an active body of its Living Head. It is perhaps therefore better equipped to reach the world on a level that will be relevant and meaningful.

Chapter 5

Beginning to build:
the meeting of church and world

'Evangelical churches are sometimes accused of being more like monasteries than mission stations.' This generalisation from Albert Wollen (*God at work in small groups*, Scripture Press p. 31) does of course, have its exceptions but it is nearer the truth than we may care to admit. The institutional church can be like a foreign land to many and equally inhospitable. The unconverted are ignorant of its form and its language.

Language

In his book *The Soul Winner*, C. H. Spurgeon confesses that he is not surprised that so many people have an aversion to attending a place of worship where the gospel is preached. He says, 'I think, in many instances, the common people do not attend such services because they do not understand the theological "lingo" that is used in the pulpit; it is neither English, nor Greek, but Double-dutch; and when a working-man goes once and listens to these fine words, he says to his wife, "I do not go there again, Sal; there is nothing there for me, nor yet for you; there may be a good deal for a gentleman that's been to college, but there is nothing for the likes of us." No, brethren, we must preach in what Whitefield used to call "market language" if we would have all classes of the community listening to our message' (Quoted by Roy Joslin in *Urban Harvest* from C H Spurgeon *The Soul Winner* Wm Eerdmans Pub Co Grand Rapids 1976 p. 93). So language can be a problem, and that needs to be addressed.

Relevance

But saddest of all, and as we have sought to show, the unconverted are ignorant of the relevance of the church. It should be a rebuke to us that in the 'ups and downs' of life the unbelieving world rarely thinks of turning to the church for help. At the end of an individual's life there may be a token recognition with a funeral service because that is right and proper, but there is no real understanding of its relevance and certainly no hope for the future. We are left with the clear impression that they have given up trying to find any answers to the fundamental questions of life from the church.

If the reason for this partition was the holiness of the church, or if you like, the 'otherness' or distinctiveness of believers, then we could accept it. Sadly that is not usually the case. There are misconceptions which unbelievers have which could have been resolved if we had kept the lines of communication open. More often than not biblical separation has been replaced by isolation and the gulf appears to be widening. We are not communicating.

How do we attempt to address our problems? Firstly the serious questions which must be asked concerning the spiritual state of the church today are as already stated, outside the remit of these pages, but they do need to be thought through and acted on. Methodology alone cannot provide the answer. Besides as Joe Aldrich points out 'God is not in the business of putting healthy babies in malfunctioning incubators.' (*Lifestyle Evangelism*. Multnomah Publishers Inc. 1981. p. 96)

Natural links

But if we turn our minds to some of the practical problems that arise for those outside our churches there are I believe some steps that can be taken. One of the most natural links that can be provided between the churched and unchurched is the home. The home is an inclusive environment where the individual is in surroundings familiar to him or her and where they are welcome for their own sake. The setting appeals to all age groups and social classes and requires no compromise of the message.

The evidence of the New Testament as we have already seen, shows that both the early apostles and later, Paul himself, were clear that even the informal situation did not bar the direct proclamation of the gospel and a call to repentance and faith (see for example Acts 16:14-15, 32; 20:20; 28:30-31).

Experience will determine the angle of approach, dependent on the type of person present and their current exposure to the gospel, but in any case, this is a situation for direct evangelism when the message can be clearly and forcefully though sensitively, declared.

Ideal hosts

The hosts for the meeting are a vital ingredient of the venture. They can be the key to success.

▶ They will have the gift of hospitality and the ability to make people feel welcomed.
▶ They will understand the philosophy behind the evening and will be sensitive to what is required.
▶ They will probably have a group of unconverted friends.
▶ They will not demand regenerate behaviour from unregenerate people.
▶ They learn the names of group members.
▶ They are sensitive to people's needs, so that ordinary things such as temperature, lighting, ventilation and Bibles are on their checklist.

The form of the meeting.

The type of meeting can have a number of characteristics. As we have already suggested:

● It can take the form of a Bible study

These can be run on a regular basis, weekly, fortnightly or monthly, or they can run as a series that covers a syllabus of some kind. They can, of course, be held on a 'one-off' basis but, whereas that may be successful with one of the subsequent ideas, in the case of Bible study it is not the best plan. If possible it is much more effective to plan a short series which will provide your visitors with an outline of the Christian faith.

The rapidly increasing framework of small groups already being arranged for believers can provide the basis for an evangelistic thrust. However, in my experience there have been some 'Bible study for believers only' groups that were unable to adapt to opening their doors to unbelievers. Though the framework was there, the group found it difficult to progress beyond the cliquishness so powerful in human nature. They were in a comfortable scenario and therefore not enthusiastic about any intrusion. This sort of group may not be ready to receive the un-churched into their company.

Joe Aldrich draws attention to another possible drawback. 'There is a big difference between an *evangelistic* home Bible study and a home Bible study. The two do not mix. I am sure you know of Bible studies where an overzealous Sister Maude or Brother Jim showed up ready to do battle. It was not long before the discussion turned from the simple ABCs of the faith to the eschatological implications of the ten horns of the beast in Daniel 7. What started out to be an evangelistic Bible study turned into a society for protecting, preserving, and propagating pet theological hobby horses. (*Lifestyle Evangelism*. Multnomah Publishers Inc. 1981 p. 164).

For this reason a Bible study group will usually be formed with an evangelistic purpose in mind from the very beginning.

Whatever the structure of the overall programme, there is no doubt that many uncommitted men and women find these groups helpful, even though they are not at this stage regularly attending church. For them this is a 'half-way house'.

Many churches have used the evangelistic home Bible study group as an introduction, which they then follow up by encouraging people to come to central mission or church meetings. It has not only relieved some of the fears of those invited, but also provided gospel input that begins to bear fruit.

The home Bible study group has also been valuable in encouraging the non-Christian spouses of church members.

Specially prepared courses for use in these situations have proliferated over the last few years. The following is a list of some sources you may like to contact:

▶ '*Christianity Explained*' St Matthias Press, P O Box 665, London SW20 8RL. E-mail mattmedia@compuserve.com

▶ '*Finding out about Christ*' Pastor Edward Challen, 642 Ringwood Road, Parkstone, Poole, Dorset, BH12 4LZ.

▶ '*Y Course*' Agape UK, Fairgate House, Kings Road, Tyseley, B11 2AA. E-mail info@agape.org.uk Web site www.agape.org.uk

▶ '*For Starters*' Pond.C 1997 Evangelical Press, Grange Close, Faverdale North, Darlington DL3 0PH. E-mail sales@evangelical-press.org. Web site www.evangelical-press.org

It is impossible to suggest resources and not mention the Alpha Course, the evangelistic tool originated at Holy Trinity Brompton, a charismatic church in London. Numerous churches in Britain and overseas have apparently benefited from it. Equally among those using it, there have been many, unhappy with certain emphases, who have made their own adjustments and still referred to it as Alpha, much against the wishes of the publishers of the course.

For a full appraisal of Alpha I recommend that you read *Falling Short – the Alpha course examined* (Hand C 1998 Day One Publications).

● It can major on a talk given by a 'professional' speaker

This person may be an evangelist or a minister who is used to this approach and will be able to make the best use of the opportunity. We should never be ashamed of this direct presentation of the Christian gospel. Many evangelists frequently speak at such events and you should not be concerned if you only expect a small number to attend. Any worthy evangelist would far rather speak to a dozen unconverted men and women in a home than to 300 Christians in a so-called evangelistic rally.

Discuss the conduct of the evening with him so that you are satisfied with the approach he will take; after all it is your friends or work colleagues he will be speaking to. In my experience men and women of the world appreciate straight talking, even if they don't subscribe to the message. The message however, should always be delivered in a gracious and sensitive, not to say polite manner.

The 'preacher' should not compromise what he says, though he should remember that he is in a living room and not a pulpit! There are things that can be said and done in a pulpit that are quite inappropriate in someone's front room. For instance it is unnecessary to raise one's voice and the language we use should be more simplified than that which we sometimes hear in church. Legitimate religious language, sometimes called 'the language of Zion,' will not help the non-church person to understand the gospel. The great truths of Scripture can be expressed just as clearly by using everyday words that people can understand. It's what Spurgeon meant by 'market-language.'

John Newton tells us how William Grimshaw of Haworth adapted the vocabulary and manner of his preaching in order to reach the 'labouring-class' people for whom he was particularly concerned. Newton says of Grimshaw, 'the desire of usefulness to persons of the weakest capacity, or most destitute of the advantages of education, influenced his phraseology in preaching. Though his abilities as a speaker, and his fund of general knowledge, rendered him very competent to stand before great men, yet, as his stated hearers were chiefly the poorer and more unlettered classes, he condescended to accommodate himself, in the most familiar manner, to their ideas, and to their modes of expression. Like the apostles, he disdained the elegance and excellence of speech which is admired by those who seek entertainment perhaps not less than instruction from the pulpit. He rather chose to deliver his sentiments in what he used to term "market language".' (Quoted by JC Ryle *'Five Christian Leaders'* Banner of Truth Trust 1960 p. 32)

An experienced evangelist will be able to adapt in a variety of ways to his audience.

● It can present the message by featuring a well-known Christian

There may be Christians in the public arena in your area who could be invited to speak about their life and work. This might be for example, in the sphere of sport, business or government. It is of particular value if their area of expertise coincides with the interests of the people you intend to invite. Non-Christians can be impressed with the Christian faith of someone who has enjoyed a measure of success in their life. The world sometimes thinks that all Christians must be 'losers' who now view their Christianity as an alternative to 'getting on' in life. In other words they believe it is impossible to be a Christian and 'successful'!

If the invited speaker addresses events like this on a regular basis, try to find out what sort of ground will be covered and whether he or she will be able to conclude with the necessary application of the gospel. If not, make sure that this is done either by you or another capable member of the group. It doesn't require a sermon but you should make sure that the 'success story' is related to the Christian faith. The aim of the evening is to show that a person can be a 'success' in the eyes of the world **and** a Christian, and that the invited speaker's personal faith is vital and relevant in their everyday life. The end purpose is that Christ should be exalted and not the guest.

Something along these lines can be particularly helpful in contacting men, who are notoriously difficult to reach.

● It can present the message through the medium of video

The home is an ideal location for this, since the television is such a familiar part of everyday life. This presents far less of a threat for some of your more hypersensitive friends. Today there are a number of excellent programmes available and these should be chosen to suit the situation.

A production from the Christian Television Association is entitled *So, who is this Jesus?* This 50-minute presentation can be broken down into three parts and has been prepared for the non-church viewer. It has been used successfully at the secondary school level and above and is a powerful presentation of the person of Christ and a most suitable evangelistic tool. It can be obtained from Christian Television Association, Wraxall, Bristol. BS48 1PG. E-mail info@cta.uk.com They have other similar videos that have been made with evangelism in mind. *So, who is this Jesus* can also be obtained from Christian Publicity Organisation, Garcia Estate, Canterbury Road, Worthing BN13 1BW. E-mail cpo@cpo.uk.com Web site www.cpo.co.uk.com

As another alternative the older *Jesus* film/video has of course been used for many years around the world and is still very effective. This can be obtained from the Agape address given previously.

Christian Television Association have also produced the series *Open Home, Open Bible*. There are four videos each containing six programmes. None of the programmes is longer than 18-minutes and they cover subjects from creation to the last things. Richard Bewes presents each programme with the help of invited guests and they are suitable for both believers and non-believers. They can also be used for personal Bible study. A workbook accompanies the series. The videos can be obtained from CPO (not from CTA) at the address given above.

Make sure that you watch the video before the evening begins so that you or someone else will know how to conclude the proceedings.

● It can be a testimony evening

This could introduce a person with an 'out of the ordinary' testimony who will share their experience of Christ with your neighbours and friends. They may have an unusual background or have been somewhere or done something a little different and they will hopefully be able to share how they came to faith or how that faith was able to sustain them.

A missionary on furlough might be prepared to come and talk about Christianity in their country and compare it with 'Christianity' in Britain. This can provide excellent material for a discussion later in the evening. Again have some idea at the beginning how you are going to end the evening.

● Other ideas

The only limit is our creativity and ingenuity, but we should always have the purpose of the meeting clearly in our mind, and recognise at all times that whatever we do, must be a suitable vehicle to carry the message of a crucified and risen Saviour.

The following list of ideas is not exhaustive!

Some years ago a popular title for a particularly honest group was **Agnostics Anonymous**. There were those that felt that the title was inappropriate but were prepared to operate more safely under the heading **Basic Christianity**. This is a very 'up-front' discussion group who will tackle head-on the major themes and difficulties of the Christian faith.

You may find that a **Recipe Swap Evening** goes down well. The invitation cards could read: 'Please bring your favourite recipe and, if possible, a sample to taste—sweet or savoury. Also a chance to hear John and Ann Appleyard talk about their forthcoming move to Africa, where John is to take up a job with a Christian relief organisation.'

A Salad Swap Evening could be run on similar lines.

A Spiritual Recipe Swap Evening can be very interesting but needs careful preparation and leadership.

People are invited to come prepared to swap ideas on what they believe 'healthy twentieth-century spiritual life' to be. It is best if they are asked to bring their 'recipe for a healthy spiritual life' written on a post card. Each person reads out his or her recipe as a prelude to discussion. The evening could conclude with a talk from a Christian, maybe on his or her job, showing how their Christian faith has affected their entire outlook on life - priorities, aims, relationships and daily lifestyle.

Meals themselves can be very good in preparing the ground but never forget the primary purpose of the evening, which is evangelism.

If you wish to invite friends and neighbours specifically for a meal when that is going to be the main feature, do so, but on that occasion don't plan a speaker. This will be valuable in building bridges, but if your plan is for evangelism then the meal is of secondary importance and you must make sure that you leave adequate time for someone to speak. It is not fair, and defeats the object of the evening, to invite a speaker and then run out of time or give him just the last few minutes of the evening. Having managed to get your friends along it would be disappointing if you missed out on the primary objective. The speaker needs time to develop his theme and at least give his hearers something to take home with them.

If there is to be a speaker, his or her part can be taken before or after the meal. Either have pros and cons and you may like to experiment to find the best format for your situation.

If you decide on a meal, the following may be helpful:

▶ Keep it as simple as possible. Two courses are adequate.
▶ You may ask those Christians attending to bring specific items.
▶ Choose a menu that can be prepared beforehand—even the day before.
▶ Keep hosts free to meet guests. Perhaps some will be strangers to each other and will need the hosts to integrate the group.
▶ Buffets are not noticeably quicker to serve than a sit down meal. In the case of a buffet it is not necessary to wait until latecomers arrive before starting the meal.
▶ If the meal is to be served at the end of the evening, make sure guests have something to drink when they arrive.
▶ If a speaker is involved toward the end of the evening, he or she can begin to speak as soon as the coffee has been served.
   Still on the subject of meals, one form of discussion style event is a

'dialogue supper'. Canon John Chapman, Director of Evangelism in the Diocese of Sydney, Australia, conceived this approach. One of the churches that adopted the idea described the evening in the following way:

'Usually a couple provide a meal for their friends (7.30-8.45 pm) followed by coffee (8.45-9 pm). The dialogue leader then gives a very direct five-minute summary of the gospel in the form "This is what Christians believe—would you like to discuss it?" Over the next two hours the basic objections to Christian belief are usually raised and dealt with . . . As the evening is usually seen as an isolated event, the gospel is central and the point of issue is its objective truthfulness rather than mere subjective relevance. So the discussion will be billed as "The validity of Christian belief" or "The uniqueness of Christ". You need a skilled leader who can handle a wide range of objections to Christian belief. Other Christians present should not join in unless invited. This approach works particularly well with students and graduates.' (ADMINISTRY resource paper 83.4: *Make yourselves at home.*)

Variety

There can be real variety as far as ideas are concerned. You should endeavour to find out what type of 'meeting' would best suit your neighbourhood, or the group you will bring together. In contrast to much of what I have said, Christians in one particular working class area found that their neighbours would come much more readily to an event held on church premises than to something in a home. They were not used to the idea of socialising in that way. This illustrates the fact that no single pattern can be imposed in every situation. One of my colleagues in introducing the 'philosophy' of Hospitality Evangelism waves a blank sheet of paper in front of his audience with this comment 'This is the programme for the mission!' Each situation demands its own model. There will always be the need to remain flexible.

The suggestions already made will show that the mood of the meeting is always low key and its conduct, simple. It majors on providing a relaxed and informal atmosphere in which to present the most important message any of your guests are likely to hear.

✪ WHO ARE WE GOING TO INVITE?

The most appropriate invitees will be unconverted neighbours, work colleagues, friends or relatives. Specifically, those people we already have some contact with—the circle of friends we already know, or should know. Our closest neighbours; those we work with or study with; relatives who know of our faith and may even respect it, but have never heard a clear explanation of it.

Incidentally, the word *neighbour* comes from a root that means 'to be near or close by.' Therefore to be a neighbour is to develop the capacity to draw near. That presupposes distance and suggests that there are obstacles to nearness. We will be recognising some of these and endeavouring to address them. Evangelism is not a raiding party or a foray into enemy territory followed by a quick retreat. It is to be someone nearby. The strategy of Jesus was to become flesh and live among us. 'The Word became flesh. God did not send a telegram….He sent a man, His Son to communicate the message. His strategy has not changed. He still sends men and women – before he sends tracts and techniques- to change the world. You may think His strategy is risky- but that is God's problem, not yours.' (Rebecca Pippert *Pizza Parlor Evangelism*. Inter Varsity Press. 1976. p. 12)

A pattern

As we have already noticed, when Christ commissioned his disciples he also gave them a pattern. They were indeed to go into the world but they were to begin where they were, in the city of Jerusalem.

The 'Great Commission' takes on gigantic proportions if we view it from the perspective of 'going into the world.'

Several years ago, an article was published in *Time* magazine about a doctor who lived through the terrible bombing of Hiroshima. When the initial blast occurred, Dr Fumio Shigeto was waiting for a bus only a mile away, but he was sheltered by the corner of a concrete building. Within seconds after the explosion, his ears were filled with the screams of victims all around him.

Not knowing what had happened, Dr Shigeto stood there for a moment bewildered, wondering how he as one man could ever handle the 'mountain' of patients. Then, still somewhat stunned, Dr Shigeto opened his black bag and began treating the person nearest to him.

When we look at the staggering needs of a dying world, we could become overwhelmed. God does not expect us to frantically try to help everyone in need. That is too big a burden. We are to do what we can and that certainly means beginning where we are.

Each of us has his own 'Jerusalem' in this particular form of evangelism. That is where we are likely to get the most positive response. Like everything else, there are exceptions and you may find some strangers will respond to an invitation, but this is unlikely. The reason why those mentioned above should be the first names on our list is because we have already begun to build a bridge of friendship with them. There should already be an existing relationship of trust. Think back on your own experience. Your own spiritual autobiography will almost certainly include an individual or individuals who provided that bridge for you.

Tom Rees wrote, 'There is no easy method of winning souls. When I first became a Christian I would spend a vast amount of time and energy putting Gospels through letterboxes and standing in the market place distributing tracts as if I were advertising a new detergent! It may be that God still guides some of His servants into this sort of activity but many years ago I learnt that usually to witness effectively, I must first prepare a man's heart by prayer, then by showing him love and friendship, win his confidence, and earn the right to speak to him about the Lord Jesus' (*Breakthrough*, p. 109).

So, do what you can, where you are and with what you have.

Redemptive friendships

In his books on personal evangelism Paul Little makes reference to 'redemptive friendships'. He saw these as respectable liaisons initiated by the Christian with the specific purpose of sharing his or her faith with another person. Without that kind of relationship, we are sure to encounter problems brought about by the current environment as outlined in the early pages of this book. It is important that those friendships are real friendships. As Joe Aldrich points out, using a fishing metaphor: 'It shouldn't be a relationship with a hook.' (*Lifestyle Evangelism.*

Multnomah Publishers Inc. 1981 p. 177). He is not suggesting that there should not be an end result in our mind; he is simply emphasising the genuineness and authenticity of the relationship.

Much as they may **need** Christ, most men and women do not **want** Christ. What they see on offer is not attractive. Giving ourselves to them can go some way to producing a change of heart in that direction. The invitation to an evangelistic event then becomes a natural progression of that friendship and is much more likely to generate a positive response.

A chorus makes clear the kind of relationship that is necessary.

'Lord lay some soul upon my heart
And love that soul through me.
That I may humbly do my part
To win that soul for Thee.'

Men and women should not merely be regarded as names or numbers but as people for whom we have a Christ-like love and in whom we have a genuine interest. Building a relationship with them will reveal whether we have a real love for them. This may take time. Their response may not be immediate but it will come. At best we can expect an enthusiastic and positive reply to an invitation to our event or a special church service. In any case they will probably feel obliged to say 'yes', and at the very least they may come simply because they just want to find out what makes us tick! Our interest in them has generated that. Floyd McClung said it well: 'People don't care how much we know until they know how much we care.'

There when needed

It is sometimes a case of 'their tragedy providing us with our opportunity'. The circumstances of life may offer us a window where we can make ourselves available to them. Life is tough, and sickness, the loss of a loved one or the loss of a job, marital problems and other pressures provide us with opportunities to express Christ's love through serving and caring for them. 'A helping hand and a sympathetic, listening spirit give your beliefs validity and impact.' (Joe Aldrich. *Lifestyle Evangelism*. Multnomah Publishers Inc. 1981 p.183). The window referred to could indeed be a tragedy, but it might just as likely be the offer we make to do some shopping, take over a meal, cut a lawn or baby sit. Equally, if we have a need, it can help in building a relationship if we let them serve us!

We should also pay attention to widows, widowers, one-parent families and those who are alone. We **must** show them that we love them and really want to help them. None of this must be acted or it will convey the reverse to what we had intended.

Some believers can display a very harsh approach as, under pressure, they push a few invitations through the letterboxes of their street and then apparently wash their hands of the matter. They seem to be indicating that they have fulfilled their responsibility and should not be expected to do more. This kind of approach for whatever reason and from whatever motive, will rarely produce a positive response. It simply increases suspicion.

What about results?

The spiritual temperature of any congregation tends to dictate the effectiveness of that church's evangelism. If only a very small minority have a desire to work in this way and others have to be press-ganged, then the ultimate result is going to be less effective.

By using the word 'result', I don't in this context mean conversion. To speak of results in the same breath as evangelism sometimes confuses God's work with ours. Let's be clear. We evangelise – God doesn't. God produces results – we don't. We are **looking** for results. We are **expecting** results, but we cannot produce them. That is within the domain of God alone (John 15:5). So the 'result' I refer to here is the positive response we can expect from the individual to our initial approach or invitation, and I maintain that this is somewhat dependent on the spiritual life of the church. Joe Aldrich would go so far as to say 'The impact of a church's evangelistic efforts is directly proportional to the health of its corporate life.' (*Lifestyle Evangelism.* Multnomah Publishers Inc. 1981 p. 18).

Evangelism is spiritual work and only spiritual people can successfully embark on it. Don't forget to ask some serious questions about where you are as a church and by definition therefore, where you are as a Christian. William Fisher writes: 'Evangelism is really the outflow and overflow of a spiritually vigorous church. Evangelism is not the cause, but the result of a spiritual church' (*The Time is Now* Beacon Hill Press Kansas City p. 69). Iain Murray has said that 'in the New Testament, evangelism is not a subject which the church has to learn; rather it is the result of the church being what she is.'

What is a successful church? It is not sufficient for a church to have a good reputation in the evangelical fraternity alone. There are churches all over the British Isles and beyond that are well known—**within evangelical circles.** Is it not more relevant to ask the question, 'What kind of reputation does that church have in its own neighbourhood?' What is the assessment of those who live within 100 yards rather than those who live 100 miles away! Is that not a far better test of a spiritual church? All of this confirms the fact that there is no easy way to reach the lost. Programme ideas and techniques are all very well, but if we don't have a heart for the sinner we will falter and fall; only the compelling love of Christ is sufficient for this work. This was Paul's own experience. 'For **Christ's love compels us,** because we are convinced that one died for all, and therefore all died' (2 Cor 5:14).

'God's redemptive love is *declared* in Scripture, *demonstrated* at the Cross, and *displayed* in the body.' (Joe Aldrich *Lifestyle Evangelism.* Multnomah Publishers Inc. 1981 p.36)

❂ WHAT ABOUT INVITATIONS

These should be attractively produced, and hand-delivered. Inferior publicity just will not do. Remember that we are trying to overcome the impression that whatever the church engages in is second-rate.

The invitation card should make it very clear what people are invited to. Their positive response to an invitation card will have been on the basis of their friendship with you. All of this will be lost if they discover you have deceived them as to the nature and content of the meeting.

I remember once being scheduled to speak at a birthday party. Just before the event I innocently asked whether the invited guests knew I was going to be there and the organiser told me that they would not have come if he had told them that! It doesn't surprise me for a moment that I am not a spectacular attraction, but I insisted that he contact everyone to explain exactly what was going to happen – even if it meant some would now excuse themselves.

Titles?

Specific titles for the talks can be helpful but they are not as important as you may think. Remember that ultimately it is not the attractiveness of the subject matter that will encourage their attendance as much as our interest in them. To read on the invitation that the speaker will present the subject 'The relevance of the Christian faith for today' will often be sufficient. However, titles that have been used to advantage are as follows:

- **Food for thought.**
- **Is anyone there?**
- **What is a Christian?**
- **What's wrong with the church?**
- **The greatest question in the world.**
- **Well, what do you know?**
- **Christianity? It's impossible!**
- **What's the best gift for children?**
- **People under Pressure.**
- **Christian answers to a world in chaos.**
- **Why read the Bible?**
- **What should a church do?**
- **What is the church for?**
- **The man born to be King.**
- **Faith. Fact or Fantasy?**
- **Will the real Jesus stand up?**

Here is an interesting fact. If women invite, then women will probably come. It is a fact that men regard anything religious as best suited for women and children. But if men **and** women invite, then it is more likely that the men will come as well. This is, of course, also dependent on the time of the meeting but certainly for an evening event let it be 'Mr. and Mrs. Smith invite Mr. and Mrs. Jones.'

Young people need not be left out. I have spoken at some excellent house meetings organised by young people who had invited their friends to something which was youth orientated. For that evening their parents were consigned to the kitchen!

On another occasion a young lady used her break from school to invite friends to her home for a simple lunch and an opportunity to hear a brief presentation of the gospel. She followed the same procedure with different friends each weekday of the mission.

In general, with your invitations, use wisdom in the cross-section of those who are invited. The company should be able to mix easily and there should be an effort to avoid tension brought about by widely differing ages or interests.

Invitation cards should contain the relevant information and be as formal or informal as the occasion requires. Use designs that provide a friendly appeal. Sometimes it is possible to have a corporate card that will cover either a number of different events at the church or alternative venues for house meetings. The relevant details for each meeting are then filled into blank spaces and this will help to keep the cost down.

Take the invitation a few weeks beforehand and make it RSVP. A phone call nearer the time will not be out of place. It can be helpful to tell them if someone else they know has already accepted your invitation. Not all respond positively but some will, particularly if we have prayed and shown genuine love and interest in them. The point has been made that some social groups do not make plans for weeks ahead but would be able to respond to something much nearer the time of the event. You must decide which is best for your area.

Numbers are not all-important but, depending on the size of room, a final number of between ten and fifteen is ideal. A larger number is encouraging and will make it possible for more to hear the gospel but it does include a downside. When too many are present, the informality may be lost and any discussion is made more difficult. Some of the previous suggestions as to the format of the evening will not work with a large attendance.

Christian friends

On the other hand, only one guest arriving can be an embarrassment for everyone. There is, therefore, something to be said for having a small proportion of Christian friends in attendance but the following should be remembered:

▶ A believer can often give an unobtrusive testimony at an appropriate point. If it is a meeting at which there has been a speaker, some of those listening will consider him to be the professional. He may even be paid to do this! A short word of testimony from a 'non-professional' can therefore be relevant and powerful. I remember on one occasion emphasising spiritual values over those things that the world generally regards as more important, and when the opportunity came for discussion, the first person to speak was a young man who was present that evening with his wife. I didn't know them but he began by saying that years before he had built up a very successful business yet had rejected the Christian faith. Due to an economic downturn he had seen his business plummet and at the same time his wife became ill. In that period of great need God dealt with them both in a powerful way and brought them to faith. This young couple were therefore able to give experimental evidence of what I had been speaking about previously, and it certainly enhanced the evening.

▶ If believers are present they must be careful to avoid any obvious distinction between Christian and non-Christian. For instance, it is not helpful for Christians to have large Bibles prominently displayed, unless the evening is specifically set aside for Bible study. Even then a smaller version might be the wisest choice. Our visitors will feel that specialists surround them, and this will spoil the carefully prepared atmosphere. If 'resident experts' take over in the discussion, then the non-Christian will realise that he is outgunned and out of place. Beware of the 'holy huddle' syndrome. In an evangelistic study group it is the non-Christian who must be made to feel special.

▶ Christians should therefore be careful about monopolising the discussion period. In many situations that time is specifically available for non-Christians to air their comments and questions, and Christians should be sensitive to the danger of taking the floor. The leader should make sure that most of the discussion involves non-Christians.

▶ A Christian should not argue or clash with the leader, even if he feels there is something he must raise later in private.

▶ Christians should not introduce controversial theological subjects, which might confuse others, particularly our guests. They might also put the speaker on the spot!

As a general rule it is as well for Christians to keep in mind that the issue under discussion is Jesus Christ, not infant baptism, total immersion, election, pretribulationalism or any other subject that in its place may be important. To this end it can even be helpful if the leader confines Bible discussion to the passage chosen and does his best to avoid moving off into parallel passages.

▶ Christians who do participate should avoid giving advice. Believers should not 'share pious platitudes and spiritual Band-aids. If they share, they should focus on their *personal experience of the truth,* not an untested list from some seminar or textbook.' (Joe Aldrich *Lifestyle Evangelism.* Multnomah Publishers Inc. 1981 p.166).

▶ Christians should be careful in their condemnation of other religions or sects. That need not mean compromising our beliefs if dealt with sensitively, but a careless and negative comment could sour the entire evening for everyone. On this point it is wise not to invite known members of other sects. Those who are deeply entrenched can be troublesome, are delighted with the opportunity to have a meeting they can address and can be totally confusing to someone who may be searching for the truth.

▶ Christians can be there to pray silently throughout the evening. This is an encouragement both to the hosts and the speaker.

▶ If it is anticipated that there are going to be real problems with a small attendance, then a few Christians can help to swell the numbers and make everyone feel more at ease. However, Christians should not normally outnumber the non-Christians. It immediately becomes apparent to the guest that almost everyone else knows each other and they are the odd one out.

▶ In morning coffee groups there will often be children present. It can be extremely useful to have a Christian or two available to look after babies and toddlers. Young mums do not usually mind their children being looked after for a while so that they can concentrate on what is being said. Orange juice, biscuits and toys can be available in another room. This is so helpful for speaker and hearers alike.

Preparations

When you have received your replies, and if you are inviting a speaker, make a list of your guests with some helpful background information on each one and send this to the speaker so that he or she has some idea of the makeup of the group for that evening. Details such as the number expected, age group, particular interests, connections with the church etc. will be most valuable to him or her.

Make sure, also, that the meetings are prayed for. Carry the names of those coming on a piece of card in your Bible and pray for them often. Try to meet with a few other believers with whom you can share information about those coming and pray for individuals by name.

Let the church fellowship know about the event and encourage prayer. Sometimes it is possible to arrange for a prayer meeting to be held at another venue but on the same evening as your event, so that Christians are praying as your evening progresses. When there has been a large programme of events some churches have arranged prayer for the 12 daylight hours or even around the clock. Individual members commit themselves to 15-minute slots throughout that period of time.

○ WHAT ABOUT THE CONDUCT OF THE EVENING?

The following are a number of suggestions that should be born in mind as the evening is in progress. They relate in particular to those situations in which there is to be involvement from non-Christians.

❯ If a Bible study is to be the central feature it can sometimes be helpful to supply the Bibles so that everyone is using the same copy and page numbers can be used. This avoids the embarrassment of those who may not be able to find their way around the Scriptures.

❯ Compliment the non-Christian on his observations. It may be familiar truth to you but to him it is brand new! Share in his or her excitement.

❯ Avoid religious clichés. Many Christians don't know the meaning of some of the words or phrases we use. How then do we expect the non-church person to understand them?

❯ It can be helpful for the leader to ask questions which do not require a direct 'Yes' or 'No' answer. We should do what we can to avoid an unbeliever being embarrassed by getting things wrong. Such questions as 'What do you imagine Jesus might have been thinking?' or 'What do some of you think?' can be much more profitable.

▶ Remember that the expectation of most non-Christians who dare to enter into anything 'religious' is to be judged and condemned. They often feel awkward, even guilty and ill at ease. 'The unchurched person often has a built-in expectation of being rebuffed. He thinks we can smell sin on his clothes.' (Leighton Ford. *The Christian Persuaders*. Harper & Row. 1966 p. 70). Unfortunately, their expectations are often well founded. Sensitive Christians will go out of their way to make the visitor feel welcomed, loved, and at ease.

▶ If a meeting for study is scheduled to conclude at a certain time, make sure that it does. It is better for things to finish on a high point, rather than endeavour to squeeze the last ounce out of the evening.

As far as timing is concerned there is no timetable that fits every situation. Children's bedtimes, school hours, work schedules, and other factors will decide what is best for your group.

For morning events the timetable can run something like this:

10.30 am	Arrive - coffee or tea
10.45 – 11.00 am	Speaker begins
11.15 - 11.30 am	Discussion begins
12 noon	Close

Afternoons can present more problems because of the 'school run' and usually best suit the retired:

2.30 pm	Arrive - tea
2.45 - 3.00 pm	Speaker begins
3.15 – 3.30 pm	Discussion begins
4.00 pm	Close

Evenings will depend on a number of factors and not least where you live. Those who commute will find it difficult to make a 7.30 pm start, whereas in other areas this may be quite acceptable. The informality of the evening means that there can be some flexibility as to the starting time and in some instances the preliminaries can begin before all are present. Certainly that can be true as far as the refreshments are concerned.

Guests should be clear as to whether they are coming for a meal or only coffee and biscuits. If a meal is served begin promptly and try to conclude within the hour. If it happens to be a buffet meal, please remember that you don't need to wait until all the latecomers arrive before starting. If you do then it will mean that everyone is at the table at the same time, with the resultant queue!

If the meal is in your home then it will be perfectly natural for you to begin by giving thanks. You may need to use more wisdom if you are in a public venue and you have unbelievers with you.

Though the planned part of the evening may be timed there is no guarantee as to when it may end, that is, unless you intend closing at a certain time and have informed your guests accordingly. If an evening has gone well, some may stay on to talk further. In any case, you may have invited them for the evening and not many events outside the church end at 9.00 pm! However, any who have to leave should be given the opportunity to do so.

When the formal part of the evening is about to begin, the host should simply, clearly and briefly, introduce the evening and the programme. If there is a speaker then he or she may lead the proceedings from that point.

Literature
It can be helpful to have suitable evangelistic literature freely available. Discuss this with the speaker.

In addition to free literature there are a wide variety of titles that will suit most types of people and you can obtain these from your Christian bookshop or church bookstall. Some books will be brief and very simple, while others will deal with the gospel in more detail. Still others will tackle specific subjects such as the authority of the Bible, the person of Christ, or the problem of suffering. Become a giver of books.

Whichever books you offer to your friends, make sure you have read them yourself and can vouch for their reliability and suitability. It might even be convenient to have a small bookstall with a good range of titles, which are there to be bought—and include some suitable Bibles. The printed page can continue to convey its message long after the speaker's voice is silent. Just beware of detracting from the main spirit of the evening and the free offer of the gospel by making it appear like a spiritual Tupperware party.

Careful preparation in all these areas will help to ensure a profitable evening, and hopefully, will provide a step in the right direction for some of your friends.

Finishing touches: follow-up

One of the outstanding virtues of this simple approach is the fact that every individual attending one of these informal events is **personally** invited, and can therefore be **personally** followed up.

First steps

This can begin immediately by asking, without any undue pressure, what our guest thought of the meeting. That may provide an opportunity for personal witness, but we should be sensitive to their mood and not push if they indicate that they don't wish to pursue the subject immediately. However, we must not be guilty of going to the other extreme and showing no interest whatsoever. They know that the evening was of special importance to us and they will expect some comment.

It is essential that we avoid giving any impression of losing interest in them, having previously shown considerable attention in getting them there. Therefore it will be important to follow that evening with something suitable to provide the next step in introducing our friends to Christ. It may be a further, similar house group. It could be an introduction to a church service and, ideally, this should be our eventual goal.

There is, of course, the possibility that there may not be an evangelical church within a convenient distance. In such a situation there is little alternative to nurturing individuals in a regular series of house meetings. This is far from ideal, except as part of a church-planting strategy. Whatever we feel is best in the individual's particular circumstances should be planned out in our minds so that we have some idea as to what the next step should be.

Persevere

Don't be too disappointed if your friend is not converted at the first meeting and even appears somewhat muddled. How many of us were converted the very first time we heard the gospel? This should spur us on to further effort. Our second greatest failure in evangelism is evident here. The first and greatest is that we don't start and the second is that, having started, we don't see it through. Many individuals are suspicious of sudden bursts of activity from their local church. In my experience, so much of the early hard work has been dissipated because we have failed to follow up our contacts in a sensitive and prayerful way. Having once got a positive response, we are not sure where to go from there. From the beginning we should be clear as to what our next alternatives could be.

Perhaps someone attending a one-off house group has said how much they enjoyed the morning or evening. That should have been the signal for the host to arrange another—but often the opportunity has been lost. Eventually, our contacts will be as difficult to reach a second time as they were the first time—and sometimes even more difficult.

We should also beware that a friendship cultivated before the event doesn't fade afterward. That will certainly plant a huge question mark in their minds concerning just how genuine that friendship was. There is the danger in the build-up to any special event that enthusiasm alone will carry us to that point, but it will be the real spiritual compassion for their soul that will see us press on. Work even harder to maintain the friendship you have cultivated.

If the church has officially sponsored the evangelistic house meeting, it can be helpful to have a supply of letters written by the minister, vicar or church leader, and personally deliver these to those who attended the meeting. This will assure them of the church's interest in them and the minister's availability, should he be needed. It might go something like the template opposite:

The letter should not push too hard but it should indicate a continuing interest and express availability.

'Harvest vehicles'

This is a phrase used by Joe Aldrich in which he rightly, I believe, lays emphasis on providing a situation in which a more direct approach can be utilised to bring our friends to faith. We will need to be sensitive to the Spirit's leading, and also to our friends' preferences and views.

Evangelistic dinners and breakfasts, church retreats, evangelistic meetings and special church services can be used in this way. A church that

St. James Vicarage
Anytown
Tel: 123456

Dear Friend

We were so pleased that you were able to accept the invitation to attend the meeting at John and Joan's home. We hope you enjoyed the evening and found some help from the subject that was presented.

If you didn't receive a copy of the booklet offered, please let me know and I will make sure that one is sent to you as quickly as possible.

We want to assure you of our continuing interest and if I can be of assistance at any time, please don't hesitate to contact me. I would consider that a privilege.

I trust we will have the opportunity of providing hospitality again before long and if you happen to be free on Sunday, the 22nd December, you may like to attend our carol service. This is always a very happy family get-together and, as well as singing traditional carols, we will be considering the relevance of the Christmas message to our lives.

It would be good to see you and if you need any help with transport, please contact me, or the person who gave you this letter.

Assuring you again of my interest,

Warmest greetings

(Rev) John Smith

Above: If the church has officially sponsored the evangelistic house meeting, it can be helpful to have a supply of letters written by the minister, vicar or church leader, and personally deliver these to those who attended the meeting. This will assure them of the church's interest in them and the minister's availability, should he be needed.

takes its evangelism seriously should schedule a number of events into its calendar for the year. It is important not to miss out on the Church festivals as ideal vehicles for a 'next step' for our contacts.

It may take a number of 'harvest vehicles' to bring your friend to the position where they can make a response. The cumulative effect is what is important.

Some may even come to the place where they will virtually ask you how they can become a Christian. Answer sensitively but directly any objections to faith, or what we might call the caricatures of the gospel. Distortions such as:

'Christianity is keeping the golden rule.'

'To be a Christian I must give up everything I enjoy.'

'To become a Christian I must go to church and attend a lot of meetings.'

For some these caricatures can be real reasons for rejecting the gospel. They need to be nailed firmly—but politely. If the non-Christian realises that Christians do have fun, then he has to remove the 'no fun' objection as an excuse. Every one of these removed may bring him nearer to the point of accepting Christ.

It is also important to underline the positive aspects of the gospel. For your friend to see and hear the results of the gospel in your married life, your business life, and your social life, is seed planting which will bear fruit. To say 'We have found that knowing Christ is a major key to our relationship as husband and wife' is a powerful and practical testimony.

All of this could lead you and him to the point where you have the opportunity of sharing the words of the gospel. It is important that we should be able to introduce our friends to a saving knowledge of Jesus Christ. For some of us this is the moment of panic. With the opportunity presenting itself to deliver personally the best news this person has ever heard we choke.

If it is a question of not knowing **how** to share, then we should ask for some help from our Pastor or church leader, in order that we may be prepared to lead them through the necessary steps to faith.

Above all we will need the wisdom and grace of the Spirit of God to discern what he is doing in their lives.

By-products of 'hospitality evangelism'

Using our home for an evangelistic purpose can produce extremely valuable side benefits.

One church said, 'Possibly the great value of evangelistic meetings, especially in people's homes, is in training the Christians to this work and making them more prepared to witness outside organised missions. We have noticed tremendous rededication and re-involvement of converted folk during and after our missions.'

That sentiment could be repeated over and over again. One minister remarked to evangelists engaged in a week of informal meetings, 'Before you came our church was evangelical—now it is evangelistic'. This surely is part of the fulfilment of the Divine plan, which is the mobilisation of the **whole** church to the **whole** world with the **whole** gospel.

It is certainly true that believers involved in active evangelism cultivate a sharpness in their Christian lives that reflects itself throughout the life of the church. Missionary strategists have remarked on the fact that where evangelism has been in decline the church stagnates. Present day Turkey, roughly the Asia Minor of the New Testament is a grim warning of this danger. Thoroughly evangelised in the first century it has now become 'the graveyard of missions' and 'a spiritual desert.' The person who said 'evangelise or fossilise' was making an excellent observation.

The evangelistic house meeting must never become a substitute for the traditional church but it can be an extremely valuable bridge to it. Our aim is to provide a helpful transition. I have tried to show in this book that, for a variety of reasons, the church is threatening and uncertain ground for many people. If we therefore concentrate exclusively on church services or meetings that look like church services, it will mean that we are ignoring the majority when it comes to evangelism.

Lawrence Richards has made an extensive study on the use of small groups in the mission of the church. He emphasises the importance of the group keeping three objectives in focus at the same time: they should encourage personal spiritual growth and mutual ministry amongst the members; they should aim to strengthen the unity and fellowship of the church and they should be mobilised for service and evangelism within the community.

David Watson comments: 'any one of these aims pursued without the others, will lead to an imbalance that could impair spiritual life and health. However, when these groups are functioning and developing along the lines suggested, they will prove one of the most fruitful means of Christian mission through a local church' (*I Believe in the Church*, Hodder & Stoughton p. 313).